The Concise Guide to
Kings and Queens

Peter Gibson

The Concise Guide to
Kings and Queens

A Thousand Years of European Monarchy

Dorset Press
New York

CONTENTS

INTRODUCTION

The *Concise Guide to the Kings, Queens Regnant, Emperors and Tsars of Europe* lists all the significant monarchs who reigned in Europe in the last thousand years. Forty-three kingdoms are examined, 688 monarchs separately identified and dated with, in most cases, biographical information. Such kings as are not included are non-starters, imposters, pretenders and over 400 minor kings in Ireland, who ruled in addition to the all-powerful ones shown.

Each country is introduced by a short history. Of the kingdoms covered twenty-one survive as sovereign states. Seven of them are still monarchies: Belgium, Denmark, Great Britain, the Netherlands, Norway, Spain and Sweden. Of those states which have either disappeared or changed their constitutions, twelve had done so by 1670, nine more by 1870 and the rest before 1970.

No duchies or principalities, no landgraviates or electorates, no counties or republics have been dealt with; though some are referred to *passim*.

Rulers' personal names provided a problem, since history is never consistent in spelling. The solution, also adopted by many history books, was to put down the name by which the King, or Queen, is most readily known. This is not always the monarch's native name. After the country entries, therefore, there is a *Conversion Table* showing the names, by which they were known in their own countries, of some 125 monarchs; names which have been 'translated' in the text.

The last portion of the book is a *Chronology* of all the rulers, showing their dates of accession, their age at that date, their kingdom(s) and the end of their reign (but not necessarily the date of their death). The list enables the reader to see very clearly what the relationships between the crowned heads of Europe was at any given moment. It also makes other statistics more easily extracted and yields largely unrealized information. To cite two examples: consider that in all the 1000 years during which forty-three countries supported nearly 700 rulers, there have only been six instances when kings of different kingdoms came to their thrones and left them in the same year as each other and only four times were two kings of the same age when they were enthroned. (The first of like *reigns* was from 1033 to 1039 when Iago of Wales ruled the same length of time as Conrad of Burgundy. The last example of like *ages at accession* was in 1481 when John became King of Denmark in May and another John, King of Portugal, the following October. Both men were twenty-six years old.)

Through its record of monarchies, many of which have disappeared, the Guide gives an idea of the changing map of Europe; the interrelationships between kingdoms and between ruling families. It gives an insight into the family feuds and conspiracies which changed the leadership of many of the countries as some moved from monarchies to republics.

ALBANIA

A Roman province for many years, Albania was subsequently administered by Normans, Serbians and Bulgarians. It then enjoyed a brief spell of autonomy before being submerged by the all-conquering Turks. The Ottoman power reigned for nearly 500 years, until the Balkan War. In 1912 Albania was declared a principality, but this proved unsuccessful and a republic was formed in 1925, a kingdom in 1928 and then, in 1939, Italy annexed the country. 'Liberated' by Italy's defeat in 1944, it took only eighteen months before a communist republic came into being in January 1946.

Capital *TIRANA*; currency *lek*

WILLIAM (1876-1945), reigned 1914. Though a Prince of Wied (a German dynasty) he was intended to be king. Deprived of all support, however, both from within the country and abroad, he left the 'throne' when the outbreak of the First World War made the situation totally impossible. He never abdicated.

ZOG, originally Ahmed Bey Zogu (1895-1961), reigned 1928-1948. By the age of twelve he was head of his clan. Upon independence being declared, the then seventeen-year-old Zog swore to uphold that independence. When Italy invaded, however, Zog and Queen Geraldine fled to Britain, taking their newly born son, Leka, with them. (It has been claimed that Geraldine had the somewhat dubious distinction of being related to one-time American President, Richard Nixon.) After the Second World War Britain refused to help Zog back onto his throne, and he went to live in Egypt. While there, he was officially deposed. He moved to the French Riviera where he died.

VICTOR EMANUEL III of Italy (1869-1947), reigned 1939-1943. He assumed the throne when the Italians overran the country, but renounced it in September 1943.

ARAGON

A small county in the north-east of Spain, Aragon was absorbed by Navarre in the tenth century. It was then established as an independent

ˈnonarchy in 1035 by SANCHO, 'The Great', of Navarre. His illegitimate
ˈon, RAMIRO, became the first king of this expanded country.

RAMIRO I (died 1063), reigned 1035-1063. He took the new throne the
year his father, SANCHO of Navarre, died.

SANCHO (1037-1094), reigned 1063-1094. He was Ramiro's son and also
Sancho V of Navarre.

PEDRO (1068-1104), SANCHO's son, reigned 1094-1104.

ALFONSO I (died 1134), reigned 1104-1134. PEDRO's brother, he was
also ALFONSO VII, King of Leon and Castile, who conquered the
Moors at Saragossa in 1118. His marriage to Urraca, a widow, was
annulled by the Pope because they were third cousins. Doubtless
Alfonso was pleased, since Urraca's morals were not all they ought to
have been. In his will he left his kingdom to the Knights Templar, but
the Aragonese chose to ignore his testamentary wishes.

RAMIRO II, 'The Monk', who reigned 1134-1137, was ALFONSO and
PEDRO's younger brother. His chosen vocation for the cloister was
delayed until the question of succession had been resolved through his
marriage and the birth of a daughter. He then abdicated and went into
the church.

PETRONILLA (1137-1163), reigned 1137-1163, the sixth and last ruler
of the Navarre dynasty. She was RAMIRO's daughter (as a result of
his obliging efforts to serve the state before he embraced the Church)
and married Ramon, Count of Barcelona.

ALFONSO II of Barcelona (1152-1196), reigned 1163-1196. The son of
PETRONILLA, he inherited Catalonia from his father, Ramon.
Aragon and Catalonia were uneasy bedfellows. Alfonso was a spare
time poet in the 'Provençal manner'.

PEDRO II (1174-1213), son of ALFONSO and Sancia of Castile, reigned
1196-1213. He was rather a puzzling person who hobnobbed in 'low
circles', yet was a brave warrior. He was killed by Simon de
Montfort's Crusaders, in a battle at Muret. An engagement sparked
off by his involvement with the Albigensians. The Saracens must have
been delighted.

JAMES, 'The Conqueror' (1208-1276), reigned 1213-1276. The son of
PEDRO II, he earned his nickname honestly, by conquering Valencia,
Murcia and the Balearic Islands, so creating a Mediterranean extension
to his kingdom. He also founded a navy to patrol it.

PEDRO III (1236-1286), reigned 1276-1285. He inherited his father
JAMES's military genius, conquering Sicily (which earned him the
epithet 'The Great') and generally stirring up matters between the
Aragonese and the Angevins in Southern Italy.

ALFONSO III, 'The Beneficent' or 'The Good Do-er' (1265-1291), the
son of 'The Great', reigned 1285-1291. He clawed back land from the
Moors, argued endlessly with the Pope and, most importantly, he
granted a *Privilege of Union* which gave his subjects the right to carry
arms.

JAMES II, 'The Just' (1260-1327), reigned 1291-1327. ALFONSO's elder
brother, he became King of Sicily in 1285, but resigned in 1291. He

then married Blanca, daughter of Charles of Anjou, hoping to patch up the family's quarrels with Naples and the Angevins.

ALFONSO IV, 'The Good' (1299-1336), reigned 1327-1336. Good he may have been, weak he certainly was. He spent more time fighting the Genoese over the possession of Corsica and Sardinia than attending to his other affairs.

PEDRO IV, 'The Ceremonious' (1319-1387), reigned 1336-1387. A man of rigid etiquette who, like his father, spent most of his life fighting battles. Pedro's battles, however, were against his own nobles whom he defeated at Epila in 1348. He also regained Sicily. He married three times: Mary of Navarre, Eleanor of Portugal and Eleanor of Sicily.

JOHN I (1350-1395), PEDRO's son, reigned 1387-1395.

MARTIN, 'The Humane' (1355-1410), reigned 1395-1410. He was the son of PEDRO, who ceded Sicily to him. Obviously a bad manager, he died without leaving a will or, in the absence of heirs, any indication who should succeed him. This resulted in a two-year hiatus after his death until a specially appointed commission met and elected a king.

FERDINAND, 'The Just' (1379-1416), reigned 1412-1416. He was the son of JOHN of Castile and King of Sicily. For reasons of his own, he supported the anti-pope, Benedict XIII. In 1415 the Emperor Sigismund persuaded him to see the error of his ways and from then on, in the interests of church unity, he supported the orthodox establishment.

ALFONSO V, 'The Magnanimous' or 'The Wise' (1385-1458), FERDINAND's son, reigned 1416-1458. He was a classicist and very much in the mould of a renaissance prince. He unwisely left Aragon to take care of itself and spent most of his time sorting out his Kingdoms of Sicily and Naples (leaving the latter to his bastard son, Ferdinand).

JOHN II (1397-1479), ALFONSO's brother, reigned 1458-1479. He was an unscrupulous, bellicose man, who quarrelled with his first wife, Blanche of Navarre, by whom he had had a son. By his second wife, Joan Henriquez (who was often thought to have poisoned her stepson) he had another son, Ferdinand. In a marriage-making master-stroke, he arranged an alliance between Ferdinand and Isabella of Castile. He thus ensured the unity of Spain, and Ferdinand became King FERDINAND V of the whole country in January 1516.

 # AUSTRIA

Originally the Eastern State – the *Oesterreich* – of Bavaria, Austria was a Duchy from the middle of the twelfth century until 'acquired' by Rudolf of

Habsburg in 1267. His descendants added bits and pieces and formed the Habsburg Empire. When the Holy Roman Empire was finally dismantled in 1806, Archduke Franz of Austria, who was the Emperor of the day, had already promoted himself to Emperor of Austria. The *Austro-Hungarian* Empire, formed in 1867, was broken up at the end of the First World War. The central section became the Austria of today and the remainder formed the basis for Hungary and Czechoslovakia, with smaller areas being absorbed by Italy, Yugoslavia, Romania and Poland.

Capital *VIENNA*; currency *schilling*

FRANZ I (1768-1835), reigned 1804-1835. He was the eldest son of the Archduke Leopold II of Austria whom he succeeded as Archduke on March 1, 1792. On April 11, 1804 he declared himself Emperor of Austria. From 1809, with Metternich by his side, Austria went from strength to strength and managed to come through the NAPOLEONIC struggles with credit (literally and metaphorically).

FERDINAND (1793-1875), eldest son of Franz, reigned 1835-1848. Sadly, he was an epileptic. His health improved slightly as he grew older and, when his father died, he was considered fit enough to rule. Luckily Metternich was still 'in the driving seat' and headed the Council of State. Ferdinand, who was sometimes, though not sarcastically, called *Der Gütige* or 'Kindly One', had some quite serious mental lapses. The revolt in Vienna forced him to take sanctuary at Innsbrück, but his health and general bearing made abdication imperative. He lived for the last 27 years of his life under close medical supervision in Prague.

FRANZ JOSEPH I (1830-1916), reigned 1848-1916. Although his younger brother, Francis Charles, was very much alive, the debilitated FERDINAND was 'guided to abdicate' in favour of his nephew, Franz Joseph. The latter seems to be remembered as a wise, patriarchal and bewhiskered old gentleman, yet as an Emperor, all he did was to sit back and watch as his empire was eroded around him. His vivacious wife, Elisabeth of Bavaria, found him kind but heavy-going. She moved to Corfu and left an actress called Katherina Schratt to look after him. (Even Herr Schratt co-operated.) In 1866 the *Dual Monarchy* was instituted, which effectively gave Hungary autonomy within the Austro-Hungarian Empire. Franz Joseph's son and heir, Rudolf, died at Mayerling, in a suicide pact with his eighteen-year-old, pregnant mistress. He left his nephew, Ferdinand, next in line to the throne. Ferdinand was assassinated at Sarajevo in 1914; an event which plunged Europe into the First World War. Franz Joseph died bemused, with his Empire on the brink of collapse.

KARL (1887-1922), reigned 1916-1918. A grand nephew of FRANZ JOSEPH, Karl was actually crowned with the ancient crown of St Stephen of Hungary in Budapest. He was to step down in November 1918, just after the end of the war that had been sparked off by the murder of his uncle Ferdinand. Though he renounced government, he never actually abdicated.

BAVARIA

A kingdom of Southern Germany, Bavaria was once the second largest of the states of the German Empire, both in area and population. The house of Wittelsbach ruled the Duchy of Bavaria from 1375, becoming electors in 1623 and finally kings in 1805.

Capital *MUNICH*

MAXIMILIAN I (1756-1825), reigned 1805-1825. He was head of the Zweibrücken branch of the Wittelsbach family and had been Elector of the country since 1799. He sided with NAPOLEON and gained further territory under the Peace of Prestburg in 1805, when he declared himself King. His French connection, understandably, gave grounds for Austrian mistrust.

LUDWIG I (1786-1868), reigned 1825-1848. Rather confusingly many reference books style all the Ludwigs as Louis. He was MAXIMILIAN's son but, unlike his father, no admirer of NAPOLEON or the French. In 1846, Ludwig became enamoured of a dancer, Lola Montez, and the scandal caused by this liaison forced his abdication. Some reports claimed that Ludwig actually married Lola.

MAXIMILIAN II (1811-1864), reigned 1848-1864. He was a liberal patron of the arts, who was obliged to ascend the throne when his father, LUDWIG, abdicated.

LUDWIG II (1845-1886), reigned 1864-1886. He was only 18 when he came to the throne. Ludwig moved his kingdom politically closer to Prussia, but neither diplomacy nor kingship appealed to him. He formed a passionate friendship with the composer Richard Wagner, settling debts of his for 18,000 *gulden* and giving him an income of 4,000 *gulden*. The King was homosexual and his personal bodyguard were chosen as much for their good looks as their military distinction. His intellect, never very strong, eventually gave way and he was declared insane in June 1886. He drowned himself five days later in Lake Starnberg.

OTTO (1848-1916), reigned 1886-1913, was LUDWIG's brother and also mentally unbalanced. His uncle, Prince Luitpold, was Regent and during the years when Otto was King in name, Bavaria shared the prosperity of Germany. Otto was legally deposed in November 1913.

LUDWIG III (1854-1921), reigned 1913-1918. The last of the Wittelsbachs and the last King of Bavaria, he was Prince Luitpold's son (and OTTO's cousin). His reign ended by his deposition on the rise of the Independent Socialists.

BELGIUM

For centuries Belgium was known as the Southern Netherlands. Its provinces, such as Flanders, Brabant, Limburg and Hainault, were once counties or duchies, often under German domination. In 1814 the north and south areas of the country united, but in 1830 the south broke away and the Kingdom of Belgium was formed under the Coburg family.

Capital *BRUSSELS*; currency *Belgian franc*

LEOPOLD I (1790–1865), reigned 1831–1865. The first King of the Belgians, he was the youngest son of the Duke of Saxe-Coburg (and a descendant of John Frederick, Elector of Saxony, who died in 1547). He married Charlotte, only daughter of GEORGE IV of Great Britain, who died in childbirth. His second wife was the daughter of King LOUIS PHILIPPE of France. Leopold refused the throne of Greece, but was *elected* King of the Belgians. He was a man of culture and judgement and has sometimes been referred to as the 'Nestor of Europe'.

LEOPOLD II (1835–1909), the son of LEOPOLD I, reigned 1865–1909. During his reign the Congo Free State was founded; a vast region autocratically administered by Leopold and used by him to feather his nest. His immense fortune was based on quite unspeakable cruelty and exploitation in Africa. His only son, the Duke of Hainault, died when he was just ten.

ALBERT I (1875–1934), reigned 1909–1934. The nephew of Leopold II, he was generally considered to have been the 'best constitutional monarch in Europe'. He died in a mountaineering accident.

LEOPOLD III (1901–1983), reigned 1934–1951. His first wife, Princess Astrid of Sweden, was killed in a car crash, but the sympathy engendered by the tragedy was not sufficient to efface his behaviour during the Second World War. Leopold personally ordered his army to surrender and he was 'kept prisoner' by the Germans. He did not return to his capital until 1950 and relinquished his royal prerogative almost immediately, to his twenty-year-old son, BAUDOUIN. He abdicated officially the following year.

BAUDOUIN (born 1930), his reign began in 1951, but he occupies a rather hollow throne. He and his Spanish wife, Fabiola de Mora y Aragon have no children.

BOHEMIA

Most of what was Bohemia now forms a large part of Czechoslovakia. Not long after it was established as a Duchy in the ninth century, it combined with Moravia as a suzerain state of the Holy Roman Empire, becoming a kingdom in 1198. It passed through various 'families' until 1562, when the Habsburgs inherited the domain. They held on to it right up until 1918, when the State of Czechoslovakia was created from part of the Austro-Hungarian Empire.

Capital *PRAGUE*

PREMISLAS I (OTTOCAR I) of the House of Premysl (1150-1230), reigned 1198-1230. There had been rulers styled as kings before Premislas: Vratislav from 1085-1092 and Vladislav II who was Elector until he became King from 1140 until his death in 1173. A state of anarchy reigned from then until 1198, when Premislas was given the formal title of King by the Holy Roman Emperor, OTTO IV, and established the dynasty for himself and his descendants.

VACLAV I (1205-1253), son of PREMISLAS, reigned 1230-1253.

PREMISLAS II (OTTOCAR II) (1230-1278), reigned 1253-1278. The greatest Bohemian king, he conquered BELA of Hungary at Kressenbrunn in 1260 and then took Austria, Styria, Carinthia and Carniola. Pride, however, went before his fall. He refused to pay homage to RUDOLF of Habsburg, was eventually forced to hand over all the lands he had conquered and was killed in a skirmish with Rudolf's forces at Marchfeld.

VACLAV II (1271-1305), reigned 1278-1305. He was PREMISLAS's son and also King of Poland from 1296.

VACLAV III (1289-1306), son of VACLAV II, he was King of Hungary and, like his father, also King of Poland. He reigned for only a year, from 1305 until 1306, before he was assassinated.

From 1306 to 1310, a form of interregnum existed. Rudolf III of Austria declared himself King, and saw to it that the following year Henry V of Carinthia, son-in-law of VACLAV II, was elected King. It was an unpopular piece of 'contrived democracy' and Henry was deposed.

JOHN, 'Jan the Blind' (1296-1346), reigned 1310-1346. He was another son-in-law of VACLAV II and the first of the house of Luxembourg to be elected king. A more or less professional soldier, he spent most of his thirty-six-year reign fighting in Italy and elsewhere. He finally met his Waterloo at the battle of Crécy. His motto was supposed to have been *Ich Dien* – I serve.

CHARLES I (1316-1378), son of JOHN, reigned 1346-1378. He was anointed Emperor in 1347 and set about making Prague one of Europe's leading cities, lovely to look at and culturally rich.

VACLAV IV (1361-1419), who was also King of Germany, reigned 1378-1419.

SIGISMUND of Hungary and Germany (1368-1437), reigned 1419-1437.

ALBERT, Albert II of Germany (1384-1439), reigned 1437-1439. He was followed by a four-year interregnum.

LADISLAS V of Hungary (1424-1457), reigned 1443-1457. He, too, was followed by an interregnum.

GEORGE of PODERBRAD (1420-1471), reigned 1458-1471. A right wing Protestant, George was unique amongst the rulers of Bohemia. Firstly, he was a true native of the country (a son of Victoria of Kunslat) with estates in the north-east, secondly, he was not a Catholic. His religion made life difficult for him and, though he made many concessions, he was usually at cross purposes with either Pope Pius II or his successor, Pope Paul II, who excommunicated him. A Catholic revolt ensued, George died and his former ally, King MATTHIAS of Hungary, took over the country.

LADISLAV JAGIELLON, also Vladislav of Hungary (1450-1516), reigned 1471-1516. He was the son of a sister of LADISLAV V, who was the first member of the House of Jagiellon to come to the throne.

LOUIS, also LOUIS II of Hungary (1506-1526), reigned 1516-1526. He was JAGIELLON's son.

FERDINAND (1503-1564), he reigned 1526-1564 and became Ferdinand I of Germany in 1556. He was the son-in-law of LADISLAV JAGIELLON.

 # BOSNIA

A region of what is today Yugoslavia, Bosnia was ruled from the twelfth until the fourteenth century by Slavic *Bans*. In 1376 it obtained its independence from Hungary, but this lasted only until 1463, when it was conquered by the *Osmanli* Turks.

STEPHEN TVRTKO I (died 1391), reigned from 1376-1391. He was a nephew of Stephen Kotromanich, a grandson of Stephen Kotroman and, for good measure, a brother-in-law of LOUIS of Hungary. He assumed the heady title, '...in Christ God, King of the Serbs and Bosnia and the Coastland' and had himself crowned with the crowns of Bosnia and Serbia, at the grave of St Sava at Mileševo.

STEPHEN DABISHA (died 1395), reigned 1391-1395. He lost Croatia and Dalmatia to SIGISMUND of Hungary.

HELENA (died 1398), the widow of STEPHEN DABISHA. She ruled from 1395-1398 on behalf of the under-age STEPHEN OSTOJA.

STEPHEN OSTOJA (1380-1418), reigned 1398-1404. He was DABISHA's nephew and possibly the illegitimate son of TVRTKO.

STEPHEN TVRTKO II (died 1443), the legitimate son of TVRTKO I, reigned 1404-1408.

STEPHEN OSTOJA reigned again 1408-1418, after his brief deposition by his more orthodox sibling.

OSTOJIC (died 1421), reigned 1418-1421. Like his father, STEPHEN OSTOJA, Ostojic was unable to hold back the rising tides of dissatisfaction amongst his nobles.

STEPHEN TVRTKO II, nothing if not persistent, came back to the throne from 1421 to 1443. He was obliged to flee to Hungary, however, after being attacked by his own vassal, Hranić.

STEPHEN THOMAS OSTOJICH (died 1461), reigned 1443-1461. He was one of the illegitimate sons of STEPHEN OSTOJA.

STEPHEN TOMASHEVICH (died 1463), son of STEPHEN OSTOJICH, reigned 1461-1463. It was his bad luck that Mohammed of Turkey personally invaded Bosnia, executed him and took over his kingdom.

BULGARIA

A *Khanate* called Great Bulgaria, populated by Volga Bulgars, broke up in the seventh century and the people moved into the region of the Lower Danube. The state formed there was annexed by Byzantium and remained so until the Asen family forged a powerful and independent kingdom. Unhappily, this country was overrun by the Golden Horde, the romantic sounding name given to the decidedly unromantic Mongols who dominated Eastern Europe in the thirteenth century. They were conquered by the Turks at the end of the fourteenth century. In 1879, after the Treaty of Berlin, the Principality of Bulgaria was created and the Coburg dynasty established. Bulgaria was on the losing side in 1918 and its Thracian territories were ceded to Greece. The country was invaded by Nazi Germany in the Second World War, and in 1944 Russia, too, declared war on the country. In 1946 the monarchy was officially abolished and a republic set up.

Capital *SOFIA*; Currency *lek*

ASEN (died 1196), reigned 1187-1196. The brothers Peter and Ivan Asen Belgun, who were Vlachs, owned the strategic fortresses at Trnovo, which controlled the north side of the country. Resentful of their masters' treatment of them, they revolted and by 1187 had broken free. Ivan was proclaimed King, having defeated the Emperor Isaac Angelos at Stara Zagora.

PETER (died 1197), reigned 1196-1197. He had ruled jointly with his brother Ivan. Then, after less than a year of sole rule, he was murdered by his own *boyars* who were probably egged on by his younger brother KALOJAN.

KALOJAN (died 1207), reigned 1197-1207. This fratricidal man was to become *Tsar* in 1204. Having disposed of PETER he began his cruel reign, during which he was known variously as *Joanitsa* and 'Whelp-John'. He conquered all Bulgaria, curried favour with Pope Innocent III (who 'loved him so much that he thought only of his interests and glory') attacked Baldwin's Crusade in 1205 and was eventually murdered at Salonika in a plot probably engineered by his Tsarina.

BORIL, reigned 1207-1218. He was KALOJAN's nephew. He reigned from December 1207 and was definitely dead ten years later, having been blinded and deposed. But the precise date of his final departure is not known.

IVAN ASEN II (died 1214), reigned 1218-1241. BORIL's cousin and son of ASEN I, he was a pious soldier and a man of genius (recognised even by the Greeks). He added Macedonia, Epirus and much of Albania to his kingdom. The Pope, however, did not figure amongst his admirers and excommunicated him.

KOLOMAN (died 1246), the son of IVAN, reigned 1241-1246.

MICHAEL (died 1257), reigned 1246-1257. KOLOMAN's brother must have been either under age or feeble, as his mother, Irene, was Regent.

MICO, a usurper, came to the throne for a few months in 1257. Although he was never recognized he could be considered a *de facto* ruler.

CONSTANTINE TICH (died 1277), reigned 1257-1277. The last of the accepted *Tsars* of the Trnova dynasty, he was killed in battle resisting the usurper IVAILO. Ivailo began his working life as a swine herd.

IVAILO, IVAN ASEN III and another IVAILO, three usurpers, occupied the throne from 1277 until 1280. This period of usurpation ended with the assssination of the second IVAILO.

GEORGE I, reigned 1280-1292. The first of the Terters, he fled after a reign of twelve years.

Two Terter usurpers followed, reigning 1292-1298. SMILITZ, a Mongol puppet King, was on the throne until 1298, when he was deposed by CAKA, a son-in-law of GEORGE, who lasted only a few months.

THEODORE SVETOSLAV (died 1322), son of GEORGE, reigned 1298-1322.

GEORGE II (died 1323), reigned 1322-1323. He was THEODORE's son and the last of the Terters.

MICHAEL SHISHMAN (died 1330), reigned 1323-1330. This first king of the Shishmanovich dynasty was killed at the *Battle of Velbuzhd* fighting STEPHEN UROSH of Serbia.

IVAN STEPHEN (died 1331?), reigned 1330-1331. MICHAEL's son reigned, for only a few months, during a confused period, when Bulgaria was harassed by Turkey and unsettled by the Serbs.

IVAN ALEXANDER (died 1371), MICHAEL's nephew, reigned 1331-1371. For part of his reign, probably between 1365 and 1371, he shared the throne with his son.

IVAN SHISHMAN (1361-1393), reigned 1371-1393. By 1371, when his father IVAN ALEXANDER was dead and he was sole ruler, Ivan was a vassal of the Turkish Sultan, Murad I. In 1389 Trvnovo fell to the Turks after a three-month siege. Ivan's death is uncertain: Bulgarian legend has him disappear in a puff of smoke during the battle of Samokov. Ivan's brother, Ivan Stracimir, defended himself at Vidin, but when it fell in 1396, the country collapsed entirely.

From 1396-1878 Bulgaria almost 'disappeared' from the map of Europe. In 1876 revolts in Bosnia unleashed political unrest in Bulgaria until the *Treaty of San Stefano*, dictated by the Russians in 1878, established the Bulgarian throne.

FERDINAND I (1861-1948), reigned 1887-1918. In August 1879 the newly-formed Bulgarian Assembly elected Prince Alexander of Battenberg, an offshoot of Hesse, as Prince of the country. He was only 22 and life was difficult. In 1886 he was seized in his own palace, forced to abdicate and political regents were appointed. In July 1887 Ferdinand of Saxe-Coburg was elected by the *Grand Sobranye* and took over, despite Russian claims that he was a usurper. He was proclaimed King in October 1908. Privately he was a respected botanist and entomologist; publicly he had great dreams of power and always wanted to recapture Constantinople 'for Christianity'. His children referred to him as 'The Monarch', but not, alas, affectionately. His country's defeat in the Second Balkan War and alliance with the 'wrong side' in 1918, forced his abdication. He died in exile.

BORIS III (1894-1943), reigned 1918-1943. Young Boris had a head start on his father, FERDINAND, in that he could actually speak Bulgarian. Though generally popular, his very right wing attitudes provoked several attempts on his life. He was the subject of a motor ambush in 1925, followed by another assault in which the cupola of the Cathedral in Sofia was brought down by explosives, crushing 200 people to death. When he did die, aged 49, it was thought that German agents had possibly succeeded where Bulgarian anarchists had failed.

SIMEON (born 1937), son of BORIS, reigned 1943-1946. He began his reign under a Council of Regents. In 1945 the Communists seized power and the young King's uncle, Prince Kyril, and over 200 other influential members of the regime were executed. A heavily rigged referendum purported to show that the monarchy was no longer welcome and Simeon went into exile in Egypt in 1946. Then followed a stint (as Cadet Rylski) at Valley Forge Military Academy,

Pennsylvania. Afterwards, Simeon married and went, with his five children, to live in Spain.

BURGUNDY

The original Burgundians were Germans who settled in the eastern part of France in the fifth century AD. They were conquered by the Franks some hundred years later. The first Burgundian King was Gundicar in 411, whose line died out with his grandson, Gundimar in 532.

RUDOLPH II, reigned 934–937, over a re-united Burgundy

RUDOLPH III (died 1032), reigned 993–1032. He was the grandson of Rudolph II, who died in 937.

CONRAD II (died 1039), RUDOLPH's cousin, reigned 1033–1039. He was also the Holy Roman Emperor, styled as Konrad II. As a result Burgundy began to lose its identity, was divided up and eventually absorbed by the French monarchy.

DENMARK

The kingdom was made up of the islands of Zeeland, Lolland and Funen amongst others, the Jutland Peninsular, Bornholm, the Faroes and Greenland. This last is an island of 840,000 square miles, over 2.1 million square kilometres. Denmark is Europe's oldest kingdom. It was unified, and the first ruling dynasty, that of Gorm, 'The Old', founded, in AD 960. His descendants ruled until 1448, when a distantly related family, the Oldenburgs, took over and have been on the throne ever since.

Capital *COPENHAGEN*; currency *krone*

SVEN I (died 1014), reigned 986–1014. He was the grandson of Gorm, 'The Old' and son of King Harald ('Bluetooth') the King who christianized Denmark. Sven was probably Harald's illegitimate son by a peasant girl, Aesa. He was also King of England for a while and actually died in Lincolnshire, in February 1014. His second wife, a Scandinavian firebrand, was the widow of the King of Sweden, who had rejected the King of Norway because she would not submit to baptism.

HARALD II (died 1019), the son of SVEN, reigned 1014–1019.

KNUT II, 'The Great' (995–1035), reigned 1019–1035. He was better known as CANUTE, King of England from 1016, *and* as Sven Knuttson, King of Norway from 1015.

HARDICANUTE (1017–1042), reigned 1035–1042. Like his father, KNUT, Hardicanute was also King of England.

MAGNUS, 'The Good' (died 1047), reigned 1042–1047. Of the House of Norway, he was also King of Norway.

SVEN II (1020–1076), reigned 1047–1076. Sven was of the House of Estrith and his mother was KNUT II's sister. He re-united Denmark and kept out intrusive Norwegians.

HARALD III (1043–1080), SVEN's son, reigned 1076–1080.

KNUT IV (1086), reigned 1080–1086. He was made a saint in 1100 by Pope Paschal II, for no apparent reason other than that he was assassinated in St Alban's Church at Odense. In 1075, when he invaded their territory, Englishmen from Yorkshire would not have considered him a fit subject for canonization. He is, however, the patron saint of Denmark.

OLAF I (died 1095), reigned 1086–1095. The brother of HARALD and St KNUT, some authorities call him Olaf IV.

ERIK I, 'The Evergood' (1056–1103), son of Sven, reigned 1095–1103. ('Evergood' is a rather free translation of *Ejegod*.)

ERIK, 'The Memorable', reigned 1103–1104. But why 'The Memorable', when he was on the throne for less than a year and was probably the illegitimate son of ERIK I?

NIELS (1063–1134), another son of SVEN, reigned 1104–1134. He was engaged in civil war with Erik and died in battle.

ERIK II (died 1137), reigned 1134–1137. He was a legitimate son of ERIK I who, to confuse matters, was also referred to as 'The Memorable'.

ERIK III, reigned 1137–1147. Probably the son of ERIK II's sister, he exchanged the throne for the cloister and retired to a monastery, leaving the country gripped by civil war.

SVEN III (died 1157), son of ERIK II, reigned 1147–1157. His throne was challenged by KNUT V, grandson of NIELS. Knut was eventually killed by Sven's soldiers, but little time elapsed before Sven's own death at the hands of VALDEMAR.

VALDEMAR, 'The Great' (1131–1182), reigned 1157–1182. He was the grandson of ERIK I, emerging as sole ruler after ten years of civil unrest. Valdemar, allied with FREDERICK, 'Barbarossa', defeated the Wends, thereby adding a Baltic possession to Denmark's kingdom.

KNUT VI (1163–1202), reigned 1182–1202. Nominally co-ruler with his father VALDEMAR, he became sole ruler in 1182.

VALDEMAR II (1170–1241), reigned 1202–1241. KNUT's brother who, like his father, extended the kingdom. Having pushed as far east as Estonia, he was captured by the Germans and finally traded his conquests for his freedom.

ERIK IV (1216–1250), reigned 1241–1250. He may have been co-ruler with his brother VALDEMAR from 1231, both were sons of

VALDEMAR, 'The Great'. He was to be killed by another brother, ABEL.

ABEL (1218-1252), reigned 1250-1252. Having eliminated his brother, he himself was killed in battle, less than two years later.

CHRISTOPHER I (born 1219), reigned 1252-1259. He was deposed by his own son's nobles.

ERIK V (1249-1286), reigned 1259-1286. He was put on the throne by a political coup, but later murdered by his very followers.

ERIK VI (1274-1319), reigned 1286-1319. Son of the murdered ERIK V, he tried desperately to restore Denmark to its strength of the days of VALDEMAR II, 80 years before. His attempts stripped his Treasury and only resulted in more violent civil war. There followed a year's interregnum.

CHRISTOPHER II (1276-1333), reigned 1320-1326. He was the son of ERIK V, but only awarded the crown when he agreed to the demands of the nobles. He later withdrew his support and plunged Denmark into even bloodier warfare, resulting in the end of rule from the throne. Duke Valdemar 'assumed power', but not the title.

VALDEMAR III (1320-1375), reigned 1340-1375. By strength of character and military acumen he ended the internal conflicts. During his expansive reign, Denmark became the leading Baltic State.

OLAF II (1370-1387), also OLAF IV of Norway, reigned 1375-1387. He was grandson of VALDEMAR III, on his mother MARGARET's side.

MARGARET (1352-1412), reigned 1387-1412. She was OLAF II's mother and 'mother of Scandinavia' as well, being Queen of Denmark, Norway and Sweden. Her control of Sweden was overturned, but Norway and Denmark remained conjoined for 400 years.

ERIK VII of Pomerania (1381-1459), great-grandson of VALDEMAR III, reigned 1412-1438. He was co-ruler with MARGARET for the last fifteen years of her life. A two-year interregnum followed his deposition in 1438.

CHRISTOPHER III (1418-1448), reigned 1440-1448. He was the nephew of Ludwig IV, Count Palatine, son of ERIK VII's sister. A member of the House of Bavaria, he was the last of the direct Gorm family.

CHRISTIAN I of Oldenburg (1426-1481), reigned 1448-1481. His descent (albeit a frail one) was from VALDEMAR I, he was the son of Dietrich of Oldenburg. He was a noted 'gilded figure', a Renaissance Man. He obtained Schleswig and Holstein for Denmark, which were to become major thorns in the country's side.

JOHN (1455-1513), reigned 1481-1513. CHRISTIAN's elder son, he married Christina of Saxony.

CHRISTIAN II (1481-1559), JOHN's son, reigned 1513-1523. The same day he was crowned King of Denmark and Norway, he was also married, by proxy, to Isabella, sister of the Holy Roman Emperor, CHARLES V. But Christian refused to give up his 'bourgeois' Dutch girl friend, Dyveke. She, poor girl, was murdered in 1517 and

Christian, himself, killed her supposed murderer. He then made Sigbrit, Dyveke's shrewd mother, his Chief Counsellor. She was universally loathed and all Denmark's troubles were attributed to the '...foul-mouthed Dutch sorceress who hath bewitched the King'. He was deposed and finally imprisoned in Kalundborg Castle.

FREDERICK I (1471-1533), reigned 1523-1533. Although CHRISTIAN II's younger son, he preceded his elder brother for religious reasons.

CHRISTIAN III (1503-1559), reigned 1533-1559. A perfervid Protestant, he was passed over for FREDERICK and never stopped opposing him. Christian founded the Lutheran Church in 1536 and, within months of acceding, imprisoned any bishop who had supported Frederick.

FREDERICK II (1534-1588), reigned 1559-1588. One of Denmark's best loved kings, and perhaps unusual in that he was one of the few Danish monarchs who did not indulge in extra-marital liaisons.

CHRISTIAN IV (1577-1648), reigned 1588-1648. Since he was only eleven when his father FREDERICK II died, his reign began under a Regency of four nobles. When he was 15, he was described as '...big set...and could speak the Dutch, French and Italian tongues...'. His court was to become one of the most splendid in Europe. Under his rule, his army and the country's defences were strengthened.

FREDERICK III (1609-1670), reigned 1648-1670. In 1660 Frederick (CHRISTIAN IV's second son) converted the elective monarchy into an absolute one.

CHRISTIAN V (1646-1699), reigned 1670-1699. The son of FREDERICK III, he was the darling of the proletariat but hated by his nobles. They were delighted when he was killed in a hunting accident in August 1699.

FREDERICK IV (1671-1730), son of CHRISTIAN V, reigned 1699-1730. Though no firebrand, he nevertheless abolished serfdom on the royal estates.

CHRISTIAN VI (1699-1746), reigned 1730-1746. His career was no more distinguished than that of his undistiguished father, FREDERICK IV.

FREDERICK V (1723-1766), son of CHRISTIAN VI, reigned 1746-1766. Like GEORGE III of England (just his contemporary) Frederick was interested in, and did much for, agriculture.

CHRISTIAN VII (1749-1808), reigned 1766-1808. One of the Danish royal skeletons in the Copenhagen closet. Having had the scantest of educations, he was brutally treated by a governor and corrupted by sexually ambivalent courtiers. Though practically an idiot, he was married to Caroline, daughter of Frederick, Prince of Wales. He was not much of a husband and the pleasures denied Queen Caroline by Christian were supplied by a German born politician, Johann Struensee. Count Struensee gradually dominated Christian, introducing many reforms to Denmark, most of them unpopular. Eventually both the Queen and her Count were arrested. He confessed to 'criminal association', the royal marriage was dissolved and Struensee beheaded.

FREDERICK VI (1768-1839), reigned 1808-1839. He had really been running the country since the 'Struensee affair' in 1772 and not doing too bad a job. He was not so successful in his dealings with the ever-so-wily NAPOLEON. As a result of abortive negotiations, Denmark was to lose most of her 'possessions', including Norway.

CHRISTIAN VIII (1786-1848), reigned 1839-1848. He was the half-brother of CHRISTIAN VII. Not a great success, he failed either to regain Norway, or stave off hostilities with Sweden. He more or less went into retirement with his second wife, Queen Caroline Amelia.

FREDERICK VII (1808-1863), reigned 1848-1863. He was much less autocratic than his ancestors, perhaps more like his father, CHRISTIAN VIII, and as diplomatically inept. Frederick failed to resolve the Schleswig problem or to produce a satisfactory new Danish constitution.

CHRISTIAN IX (1818-1906), reigned 1863-1906. He was the son of William, Duke of Schleswig Holstein-Holstein-Sonderburg-Glücksburg and greatgrandson of FREDERICK V. A modest man who lived in a modest way, his children were to colour the royal families of Europe. Frederick married the daughter of the King of Sweden, GEORGE became King of Greece, Alexandra married EDWARD VII of England, Dagmar was the Tsarina of Russia and Tyra married the Duke of Cumberland. His grandson became HAAKON VII of Norway in 1905.

FREDERICK VIII (1843-1912), reigned 1906-1912. During his reign, Iceland gained independence from Denmark, but retained a 'personal union' with the mother country.

CHRISTIAN X (1870-1947), reigned 1912-1947. In 1915 Danish women were given the right to vote – such measures were typical of the reign of this much-loved king. His courage and bearing under the stress and indignity of the German occupation of Denmark during the Second World War, were admirable. In 1943 he was imprisoned by the Nazis in his own castle at Amalienborg.

FREDERICK IX (1899-1972), son of CHRISTIAN X, reigned 1947-1972. In 1953 (in agreement with his brother Knud) Frederick reopened the throne to admit Queens Regnant. The move was significant as Frederick and his Queen (Ingrid of Sweden) only had two daughters.

MARGRETHE II (born 1940), her reign began in 1972. In 1967 she married Count Henri de Laborde de Monpézat, a French diplomat. By 1969 she had given birth to two sons, the heir, the Crown Prince Frederick, and Joachim.

ETRURIA

Also called *Tuscia* hence the modern Tuscany, which was the northern part of this ancient kingdom. When the French expelled Ferdinand in 1800, the Grand Duchy of Tuscany was restyled as the Kingdom of Etruria and bestowed by NAPOLEON on the Crown Prince of Parma in 1801.

Capital *FLORENCE*

LOUIS I (1773-1803), reigned 1801-1803. The Grand Duke of Tuscany, whose family had ruled the duchy since 1531, was dispossessed by the French not long after they marched into Florence in March 1799. NAPOLEON then gave the throne to Louis of Parma. (Parma, a duchy of northern Italy, had been ceded to the Bourbon, Don Philip of Spain, in 1748.)

LOUIS II (1799-1849), reigned 1803-1808. The son of LOUIS I and also Charles, Duke of Parma, his reign only lasted just over four years. Upon the throne being given up, the Grand Duchy was re-invoked but, instead of being handed back to Ferdinand's family, it went to NAPOLEON's sister, Elizabeth, by then Princess of Lucca. In 1814 Ferdinand was restored, Lucca united with Tuscany and the whole state was annexed by the Kingdom of Italy in 1860.

FRANCE

Today the largest state in Central Europe, the Kingdom of France really emerged as a result of the Carolingian Empire's disintegration. The last Carolingian, Louis V, who was killed in a hunting accident in 987, was succeeded by Hugh Capet, whose descendants ruled the kingdom until 1328. For centuries the power of the French Kings was far from consolidated in their own realm. This situation was underlined in 1340 when EDWARD III of England began to style himself *Rex Angliae et Franciae*; then in 1420 HENRY V called himself *Regens Franciae*.

Capital *PARIS*; currency *French franc*

ROBERT II, *Le Pieux* (970-1031), reigned 996-1031. He had been joint ruler with his father Hugh, the first Capet, who died in 996. The reign was bedevilled by famine throughout the land and revolution.

HENRI I (1011-1060), reigned 1031-1060. His father, ROBERT, with whom he shared the throne for five years, very unwisely gave Burgundy to Henri's brother, Robert.

PHILIPPE I (1053-1108), reigned 1060-1108. He succeeded at the age of seven and by the time he was fourteen he was 'ruling in his own right'.

LOUIS VI (1081-1137), who reigned 1108-1137, was variously nicknamed 'The Fat', 'The Wideawake' and even 'The Bruiser'. Luckily the army was on his side and he was able to enlist its support against his step-mother, Bertrada, who tried to poison him.

LOUIS VII, *Le Jeune* (1120-1180), reigned 1137-1180. The son of LOUIS VI, he took part in the Second Crusade, which proved a disaster for him. His first wife, Eleanor of Aquitaine, married HENRY II of England. She complained that Louis was 'more like a monk than a king'.

PHILIPPE II, 'Augustus' (1145-1223), son of 'Le Jeune', reigned 1180-1223. He banished Jews from his kingdom and went on a Crusade (which proved more successful than his father's) with RICHARD I of England. In 1190 he was able to take possession of Normandy, Anjou, Maine and Poitou, followed by Touraine.

LOUIS VIII, *Le Lion* (1187-1226), reigned 1223-1226. He combined ability as a soldier with a certain religious quality. In 1216 he was offered the throne of England by a group of English barons, who were disenchanted with King JOHN. He actually invaded England, despite the manoeuvre being banned by the Pope. In any case his invading force was defeated at the *Fair of Lincoln*. He later went on the Albigensian Crusade and helped direct the brutal massacre at Marmande.

LOUIS IX, Saint Louis (1215-1270), reigned 1226-1270. A son of *Le Lion* he was canonized in 1297. He went on the 1249 Crusade and captured Damietta, but shortly afterwards the Ayoubite Sultan captured the entire French army. Louis was imprisoned and spent four years captive in Syria. Between this time and 1269, when Louis set off on a second Crusade, France enjoyed a sort of minor *golden age*. Upon returning to France Louis subdued his nobles and made peace with HENRY III of England and JAMES of Aragon. Domestic affairs settled, he sailed for Africa, but died of the plague at Carthage.

PHILIPPE III, *Le Hardi* (1245-1285), reigned 1270-1285. He was the second son of LOUIS IX. He added Toulouse to France in 1271, only to die fighting in Aragon.

PHILIPPE IV, *Le Bel* (1268-1314), reigned 1285-1314. Handsome, cynical and detached, this son of *Le Hardi* made many changes in France, quarrelled with the Pope and persecuted French Jews.

LOUIS X, *Le Hutin* (1289-1316), reigned 1314-1316. Louis was as stupid as his father, PHILIPPE, was good-looking. In 1305, he inherited Navarre from his mother, Joan. He died on June 5, when his second wife, Clemence of Hungary, was four months pregnant. During the remaining months of the pregnancy there was an interregnum until, on November 14, a boy, JOHN, was born. Five days later he died, so his uncle, LOUIS X's brother, took the throne.

PHILIPPE V, *Le Long* (1293-1322), reigned 1316-1322. He finally ended the war in Flanders. He also successfully opposed the claims to the throne of his niece Jeanne, the daughter of LOUIS X. In doing so he established the fundamental difference between the French and the other European monarchies: that no woman could reign in France.

CHARLES IV, *Le Bel* (1294-1328), reigned 1322-1328. He was the last of the House of Capet. After his death there was another interregnum, during the last three months of his widow's pregnancy. A daughter was born and denied the throne as a result of her uncle's edict.

PHILIPPE VI (1293-1350), reigned 1328-1350. He was the first of the House of Valois and a nephew of PHILIPPE IV. He ruled during a bad time for France: in 1340 the plague had ravaged Europe, in 1346 EDWARD III of England defeated him at Crécy and the French navy was destroyed at Sluys.

JOHN II, *Le Bon* (1319-1364), reigned 1350-1364. PHILIPPE's son, he was captured at Poitiers by the English and taken to London as hostage. In 1360 he was permitted to return to try and raise the ransom. The hostage who took his place broke *parole* and John, a true gentleman, returned to London, where he died, still a prisoner.

CHARLES V, *Le Sage* (1337-1380), reigned 1364-1380. He recovered much of the territory lost to the English by his grandfather, PHILIPPE VI.

CHARLES VI (1368-1422), reigned 1380-1422. During his reign civil war was rife and then, in 1415, the English army, under HENRY V, totally defeated the French forces. Charles became wholly insane and suffered from the extremely inhibiting fixation that he was made of glass and therefore breakable if moved.

CHARLES VII (1403-1461), reigned 1422-1461. The son of CHARLES VI, he was not actually crowned King until 1429. During his reign the so-called *Hundred Years War* at last came to an end. With Joan of Arc's victories, national morale expanded and the English were left with only a toe-hold at Calais.

LOUIS XI, 'The Spider' (1423-1483), reigned 1461-1483. He established an absolute monarchy, but the last years of his life were made miserable by his obsessive fear of death. In the last tortured months, it was said, he drank warm blood from infants, hoping to stave off the Reaper.

CHARLES VIII (1470-1498), son of LOUIS XI, reigned 1483-1498. He just failed in his attempt to add the Kingdom of Naples to his territory.

LOUIS XII (1462-1515), reigned 1498-1515. The first of the Valois-Orleans dynasty and often called 'The Father of His People', he was great-grandson of CHARLES V and son-in-law of LOUIS XI.

FRANCIS I (1494-1547), brother of LOUIS XII, he reigned 1515-1547. A literate, athletic young man; he was a patron of the arts who was sufficient of a soldier to triumph in the Italian war and win Burgundy for France.

HENRI II (1519-1559), reigned 1547-1559. The son of FRANCIS, he was mortally wounded in a joust.

FRANCIS II (1544-1560), reigned 1559-1560. The eldest, if short-lived, son of HENRI II, whose wife was MARY, Queen of Scots.

CHARLES IX (1550-1574), reigned 1560-1574. He was a mentally deficient youth. On St Bartholomew's Eve, 1572, he was forced by his ogress of a mother, Catherine of Médici, to order the massacre of over 3,000 French Protestants.

HENRI III (1551-1589), reigned 1574-1589. He had been elected King of Poland in May 1573, but fled when his brother CHARLES providentially died. The Catholic League found even his relatively rigid anti-Protestant stance too conciliatory and he was assassinated while beseiging Paris, by a monk, called Jacques Clément. He was homosexual and was believed to have practised 'Black Magic'.

HENRI IV (1553-1610), reigned 1589-1610. The first Bourbon, he was also King of Navarre from 1562 and a distant descendant of LOUIS IX. He was a strong king, but had '…the morals of an alley cat'. He was eventually assassinated by a Catholic, Ravaillac.

LOUIS XIII, *Le Juste* (1601-1643), reigned 1610-1643. A poorly child, he quarrelled with his mother, the formidable Marie de Médici, who was Regent. Eventually he appointed Cardinal Richelieu as his Chief Minister.

LOUIS XIV, *Le Grand* or *Dieudonné* (1638-1715), reigned 1643-1715. He was the son of LOUIS XIII. Cardinal Mazarin was his mentor and his reign has sometimes been referred to as France's *Augustan Age* and Louis himself called 'The Sun King'. Yet, by forcing his ruling classes to become little more than lackeys at his court, he sowed the seeds of republicanism.

LOUIS XV, *Le Bien-Aimé* (1710-1774), reigned 1715-1774. Too well-beloved perhaps: in five years he was reputed to have given *one* of his mistresses, Madame du Barry, *180 million livres*. During his reign, France 'lost' Canada, sold Louisiana and the revolution came one step nearer. His constitution could not match his libido, so '…after a life of vice, he was seized by small pox and died unwept'.

LOUIS XVI (1754-1792), grandson of LOUIS XV, reigned 1774-1792. The pigeons came home to roost. The third Estate declared itself a National Assembly and a Republic was declared on September 21, 1792. Louis and his family were imprisoned and he and his Queen, the Austrian Marie Antoinette, were both beheaded.

LOUIS XVII (1785-1795), reigned 1793-1795. The small son of LOUIS XVI, he was declared King by exiled Royalists in January 1793. He died, still a prisoner, in the *Temple* in June 1795. He was never crowned and can hardly be counted as King of France.

The Convention ran the country from 1792 until October 1795, when the Directorate, a five-membered body, took over the country's government until 1799. In November of that year the first of the Consuls was appointed. The last consul, Charles François Lebrun, handed over to NAPOLEON on May 18, 1804.

THE FIRST EMPIRE

NAPOLEON BONAPARTE (1769-1821), reigned 1804-1815. 'The Little Corporal', he was only about five feet two inches (157 centimetres) tall and had once been an army corporal. He came from a large, Corsican family, but by combining his brilliance with ruthlessness he rose to be the most powerful man in Europe. His generalship was masterful and he subdued the armies of practically all France's neighbours in a few years, even extending French dominion into Egypt. His career began to take a downward course when his armies were heavily defeated in both Russia and Spain. He abdicated on April 6, 1814 and went into exile on Elba. On March 20, 1815, he was restored. But on Sunday June 18, 1815, at the end of *The Hundred Days* he was defeated by the Allies under the Duke of Wellington at the *Battle of Waterloo*. He was exiled to the island of St Helena where he died (some suspected poisoned) six years later. Despite his tyrannical rule, Napoleon restored order to France, gave the country a Legal Code and established the National Bank.

LOUIS XVIII (1755-1824), reigned 1815-1824. He was the brother of the decapitated LOUIS XVI, who assumed the title of King in 1795. He 'ruled' from April 1814 to March 1815 and then re-established the Bourbon dynasty after NAPOLEON's final downfall. His last words were popularly supposed to have been, 'A King should die standing'. An interesting death bed comment from an obese man of 69, suffering terribly from gout.

CHARLES X (1757-1836), reigned 1824-1830. LOUIS XVIII's brother, he had been living in Scotland. He brought a reactionary outlook to the throne and set about compensating the nobility for their losses in the Revolution. This totally misjudged action caused another revolution and his abdication.

LOUIS XIX (1775-1844), he reigned on August 2, 1830, from breakfast until tea-time, making history by being the shortest reigning king on record. Upon the abdication of his father, he succeeded to the throne in the morning, but abdicated later the same day.

HENRI V (1820-1883), reigned in 1830. A contender for his uncle LOUIS XIX's record; Henri reigned from August 2 to August 9. He was the last of the Elder Bourbon line.

LOUIS-PHILIPPE, *Le Roi-Citoyen* (1773-1850), reigned 1830-1848. He was the great-great-great-great-grandson of LOUIS XIII, so not all that *bourgeois*. Though elected, he became so unpopular through his repressive regime that he was dethroned by yet another revolution. He died, a sedate 77, in England.

The Provisional Government of February 1848 gave way to the Constituent Assembly in June, after riots in Paris. The President, Prince Louis Napoleon, nephew of NAPOLEON I, led the body until December 1852.

THE SECOND EMPIRE

NAPOLEON III *(1808-1873)* reigned 1852-1870. The ex-President and only surviving son of Louis Bonaparte, quondam King of Holland. This womanizing, wax-moustachioed, tinpot Emperor staged a coup on the anniversary of the *Battle of Austerlitz* and, having suppressed opposition, proclaimed the Second Empire, Never popular, the humiliation of the country in the Franco–Prussian War eliminated any residual support and he was deposed.

The Third Republic was proclaimed on September 4, 1870.

 # GERMANY

The Romans controlled land now covered by the south and west of the country; the remainder was ruled by a number of German tribes. After the decline of Rome, the Franks, the Agilulfings and the Carolingians divided the country between them, until the Holy Roman Empire was created by Charlemagne in 800. By the early part of the second millenium, Germany was a powerful force, but split into a number of increasingly important duchies and minor states, such as Saxony, Swabia and Franconia. By the sixteenth century the Habsburgs ruled the roost. True national unity was not achieved until 1871, when the German Empire was created. After the Second World War, Germany was redivided; one part is the Federal Republic, established in September 1949, which obtained complete autonomy in May 1955. The other side of the division is the Democratic Republic, dominated by the USSR, the capital of which is East Berlin.

Capital of the Federal Republic *BONN*; currency *Deutschemark*

(HRE) after a king's name, means he was also Emperor of the Holy Roman Empire.

OTTO III (980-1002), reigned 983-1002 (HRE). The son of Otto II, he was chosen as his father's successor in 983, six months before Otto II actually died. Early in 984 the little King was seized by Henry, deposed Duke of Bavaria, but eventually handed back to his mother, Theophano. He was declared 'of age' in 995, crowned the following year and ruled without a Regent. A precocious boy, he was sometimes called 'The Wonder of the World'. He died whilst on a military campaign against the Romans.

HENRY II (973-1024), reigned 1002-1024 (HRE). He was the great-grandson of Henry, 'The Fowler' of Bavaria and called 'The Holy' or 'The Lame'. It was often supposed that he wanted to be a monk and posthumous legend claimed that he had a 'celibate marriage'. His wife, Cunegund, would probably have disagreed, however. Henry founded the See of Bamberg and was canonized for this act of episcopal piety in 1146. His sanctity was emulated by Cunegund, who became a saint in 1200. Both Henry and she were ardent supporters of Benedictine monasticism.

CONRAD II of Franconia (990-1039), a grandson of Otto the Great, reigned 1024-1039 (HRE).

HENRY III, 'The Black' (1017-1056), Conrad's son, reigned 1039-1056 (HRE). In his reign the Holy Roman Empire was extended to include Hungary, most of southern Italy and Bohemia.

HENRY IV (1050-1106), reigned 1056-1106 (HRE). In 1065 he was declared of age and a year later proved it by marrying Bertha of Savoy. 'After a licentious youth', he later developed considerable (and very necessary) diplomatic skills. He had to deal not only with irritated Popes, by one of whom he was excommunicated, but with no less than three usurpers, or Anti-Kings, Rudolf, Herman and his own son, Conrad (details under Holy Roman Empire) and a faithless second wife. His usurping son finally took him prisoner and he was forced to abdicate in 1105. He escaped from custody and was trying to rally aid from England, France and Denmark when he died at Liège.

HENRY V (1086-1125), reigned 1106-1125 (HRE). The younger son of HENRY IV, his reign was beset with difficulties from the start – from within his family, his kingdom and the Papacy. He married MATILDA, daughter of HENRY I of England, in 1114 and lived long enough to see her recognized as heir presumptive to the English throne.

LOTHAIR III of Supplinburg, 'The Saxon' (1075-1137), reigned 1125-1137 (HRE). He was an elected King.

CONRAD III of Hohenstauffen (1093-1152), reigned 1138-1152 (HRE). The grandson, by female descent, of HENRY IV, he was never actually crowned.

FREDERICK, 'Redbeard', *Rotbart* (1123-1190), nephew of CONRAD, he reigned 1152-1190 (HRE). Whether by flattery, in the bestowal of titles or by flattening on the field of battle, 'Redbeard' brought Germany to heel and (temporarily at least) restored his imperial authority in the cities of Lombardy. Satisfied with matters on the home front, he set off on the Third Crusade and was drowned in Kalykadnos the following year.

HENRY VI, 'The Cruel' (1165-1197), reigned 1190-1197 (HRE). The son of 'Redbeard', he was also King of Sicily.

PHILIP (1177-1208), another of 'Redbeard's' sons, he reigned 1198-1208 (HRE). He was elected but never crowned so, technically, never king. In the ten years of his 'reign', before being assassinated, he was constantly at war with OTTO, Duke of Saxony, the second son of Henry, 'The Lion'.

OTTO IV of Saxony (1174-1218), reigned 1198-1215 (HRE). His grandfather was HENRY II of England, his daughter, Maud, married 'The Lion'. He was probably born at Argenton in France and King

RICHARD I of England made him Duke of Aquitaine. Both civil war and foreign campaigns made for a busy reign, but he eventually withdrew to his Brunswick domain, after being defeated at Bouvines in 1214.

FREDERICK II of Sicily (1194–1250), reigned 1215–1250 (HRE). The son of HENRY VI, he was also King of Sicily. During his reign he had to contend with two Anti-Kings who were both simultaneously Holy Roman Emperors, Henry Raspe and William II of Holland.

CONRAD IV (1218–1254), reigned 1250–1254 (HRE). He was the son of FREDERICK and never crowned, but nevertheless King of Sicily. He was followed by an interregnum.

RICHARD of Cornwall (1209–1269), he reigned in 1257 (HRE). The second son of King JOHN of England, he was elected but never crowned. He married three times, the last time when he was over 60.

ALFONSO X of Leon and Castile (1221–1284), reigned 1257–1273 (HRE). Again someone who was elected but not crowned, so technically not a king.

RUDOLF, Duke of Austria (1218–1291), reigned 1273–1291 (HRE). He was the first of the Habsburgs and elected but never crowned. He was followed by another short interregnum.

ADOLF (1250–1298), reigned 1292–1298 (HRE). He was the son of Walram, Count of Nassau. Another of the elected, uncrowned brigade, he owed his election more '...to the political conditions of the time than his personal qualities'. His electoral promises were not honoured and ALBERT of Austria was elected King. The rival monarchs met at Göllheim in July and Adolf died there, probably murdered by ALBERT's followers.

ALBERT I (1250–1308), reigned 1298–1308 (HRE). The son of RUDOLPH, he was a stern man who, unusually for his day, had considerable sympathy for the serfs and offered protection to persecuted Jews. This side of him does not seem to have been in evidence in Switzerland, where he is remembered as despicable and cruel. He was murdered by his nephew, John (afterwards, incorrectly, called 'The Parricide') whilst on his way to suppress yet another revolt.

HENRY VII (1270–1313), reigned 1308–1313 (HRE). He was also Henry IV of Luxembourg. He died in Italy, on his way to attack Naples in fact, but had obviously already made his mark in Italian literary circles. Dante honoured him in his poem *Il Paradiso*. There followed a short interregnum.

LUDWIG, the Bavarian (1286–1347), reigned 1314–1347 (HRE). He found himself in opposition to the Anti-King, Frederick, 'The Fair' of Austria, whom he took prisoner during the *Battle of Mühldorf* in 1322.

CHARLES IV of Luxembourg (1316–1378), reigned 1347–1378 (HRE). He was the son of JOHN, King of Bohemia. In 1356 he published the *Golden Bull* (so called because of its golden seal) which laid down the rule by which a Holy Roman Emperor could be elected. He thus managed to extract the institution from the grasp of the Vatican. In 1349 Charles had to cope with the Anti-King Günther.

VACLAV (1361-1419), reigned 1378-1400 (HRE). The son of CHARLES, he was deposed from the German throne in 1400, but allowed to continue as VACLAV of Bohemia. In the last year of his German reign, FREDERICK of Brunswick-Luneburg, an anti-king, made his brief appearance.

RUPERT III of the Palatinate (1352-1410), reigned 1400-1410 (HRE). (Frederick, Duke of Brunswick, had been elected, but was assassinated immediately after the votes had been counted.)

SIGISMUND (1361-1437), reigned 1410-1437 (HRE). The son of CHARLES and brother of VACLAV, he was also King of Bohemia and Hungary. During his reign, John Huss, the Bohemian religious reformer, was burned to death as a heretic at Constance, despite having been given a personal 'safe conduct' by Sigismund. The last of the Anti-Kings, Jobst of Moravia, made his appearance during the first year of Sigismund's reign.

ALBERT II (1397-1439), reigned 1437-1439 (HRE). He was also Albert V of Austria, the great-great-grandson of ALBERT I and King of Bohemia and Hungary. A short interregnum followed his rule.

FREDERICK III (1415-1493), ALBERT's brother, reigned 1440-1493 (HRE). On March 16, 1452, he married Leonora of Portugal in Rome and three days later he was crowned Emperor of the Holy Roman Empire by Pope Nicholas V. He was the last Emperor to go to Rome for his coronation, all his successors assumed the title immediately upon their election.

MAXIMILIAN (1459-1519), reigned 1493-1519 (HRE). He was FREDERICK's son and Archduke of Austria. In 1495 he declared a *Perpetual Peace* (as likely, one imagines, as 'Perpetual Motion') and divided Germany into six parts. In 1513, assisted by HENRY VIII of England, he defeated the French at Guinegate, in the *Battle of the Spurs* a reference to the precipitate flight of the French, who spurred their horses from the field.

CHARLES V (1500-1558), reigned 1519-1556 (HRE). The son of Philip of Austria and Joan of Castile, he had ruled Spain as CHARLES I since 1516. An ill and nervous man, he abdicated from all his kingdoms in 1555 and 1556 and retired to a monastery at Yuste in Spain. (It was during his reign that the Spaniards conquered Mexico and Peru.)

FERDINAND I (1503-1564), brother of CHARLES, reigned 1556-1564 (HRE). In 1521 he married Anna. In 1526, on the death of his brother-in-law, LOUIS, he was elected to the thrones of Bohemia and Hungary. He and Charles inherited the Austrian dominions in 1519, but he handed his shares to his brother three years later.

MAXIMILIAN II (1527-1576), reigned 1564-1576 (HRE). He was a mild, ecumenically-minded son of FERDINAND. He negotiated a treaty with Selim of Turkey in 1568 and brought a degree of peace to the Roman Empire.

RUDOLF II (1552-1612), son of MAXIMILIAN, reigned 1576-1612 (HRE). He was scholarly, absent-minded and very much the puppet of the court of Spain. He gave the Bohemian Protestants their religious freedom in 1609 and conceded the Hungarian throne to his younger brother, MATTHIAS, two years later.

MATTHIAS (1557-1619), reigned 1612-1619 (HRE). A far more worldly man than his elder brother RUDOLF, he plotted against him continuously. He had no legal children and so, having acquired the Hungarian throne, he arranged for his cousin FERDINAND of Styria to succeed him.

FERDINAND II (1578-1637), reigned 1619-1637 (HRE). He was MATTHIAS's cousin and fellow 'throne fixer'. Their joint machinations rebounded on him and he was deposed from the Bohemian throne by Protestant elements, in 1619. He took his revenge a year later and virtually 'abolished' the religion.

FERDINAND III (1608-1657), reigned 1637-1657 (HRE). He succeeded his father, FERDINAND II, as Holy Roman Emperor and King of Germany, Hungary and Bohemia, having been an involved witness to the total defeat of the Swedish army at the *Battle of Nördlingen* three years before.

LEOPOLD I (1640-1705), reigned 1658-1705 (HRE). FERDINAND's second son, he spent most of his forty-seven-year reign at war. Through his Spanish family connections he became caught up in the *War of Spanish Succession* which had a profound effect on the history of Europe as a whole and on its monarchies in particular. The war arose out of a dispute over who should succeed CHARLES II. It waged from 1701 until 1713, when it was finally settled by the *Peace of Utrecht.*

JOSEPH I (1678-1711), reigned 1705-1711 (HRE). LEOPOLD's son carried on the *War of Spanish Succession* though he did not live to see its conclusion as he died of smallpox in Vienna, when he was only 32.

CHARLES VI (1685-1740), reigned 1711-1740. He was JOSEPH's brother and, as CHARLES III, Pretender to the Spanish throne. In 1713 he issued a *ukase* now called *The Pragmatic Sanction*. It decreed that all Austrian territory should remain undivided and, if there were no male heirs, that these lands should devolve upon his daughters, which, importantly in this case, meant his daughter MARIA THERESA.

MARIA THERESA (1717-1780), reigned 1740-1780. Her right to the throne was supported by England (the right having been stipulated in her father, CHARLES's, *Pragmatic Sanction*). She was, of course, now Archduchess of Austria and probably contributed more than any other man or woman to the creation of modern Austria. Her grandson, FRANZ, was created Emperor of Austria in 1806, the year the Holy Roman Empire ceased to exist. She ruled Austria alone from October 1740 until August 1765 and jointly with her eldest son, Joseph II, father of FRANZ, until her death.

GERMAN EMPIRE

In 1871 the Hohenzollern family, who controlled practically all northern Germany, brought all the different states together and formed a united kingdom for the first time. WILLIAM I, a Hohenzollern, who had been King of Prussia for ten years, was persuaded to accept the title of Emperor. It was against his better judgement, for, unlike his grandson WILLIAM II, he had little use for titles. All three Emperors retained the subsidiary title of King of Prussia.

WILLIAM I (1797-1888), reigned 1871-1888. He had been King of Prussia since 1861. As a young man, and a Captain in the army, he was awarded the *Iron Cross* for bravery shown at Bar-sur-Aube in 1815. Politically he was an ultra-Conservative; a suitable outlook for a German Field Marshall in 1854. Four years later he became his brother's Regent. He had a good friend in Bismarck and any impetus the Emperor lacked may have been counterbalanced by Bismarck's not entirely discreet encouragement. It was during the siege of Paris that William announced the adoption of his title, Emperor of Germany, and in March 1871, he opened the first Imperial Parliament.

FREDERICK III (1831-1888), reigned in 1888. In contrast to his father, WILLIAM, Frederick was very much a Liberal. He married the Princess Royal, eldest daughter of Queen VICTORIA of England, in 1858. He was understandably opposed to Bismarck and the policies fostered by that political prince. In his early fifties Frederick developed cancer of the throat and became mortally ill. An English throat specialist, Morell Mackenzie, was summoned, over the heads of the Crown Prince's medical advisers. Mackenzie was unable to prolong his royal patient's life, indeed, through his ineptitude, he probably shortened it. By the time his ninety-year-old father, WILLIAM, had breathed his last in Berlin on March 9, Frederick had only days to live.

WILLIAM II (1859-1941), reigned 1888-1918. In 1901 Queen VICTORIA, his grandmother, died in his arms – literally. Yet just over 13 years later, he led his country in war against his cousin, GEORGE V, another of Victoria's grandchildren. William was born with a foreshortened left arm. Amateur psychologists would no doubt argue that he compensated for this disability by an over aggressive attitude and a passion for military uniforms and splendid regalia. William blamed his advisers for the First World War and it is recorded that on August 1, 1914, as he signed the order for German mobilization, he said to the Assembly, 'Gentlemen, you will live to rue the day that you made me do this'. Whether or not they did is moot; he certainly did. On November 10, 1918, the Emperor William slipped into Holland and became a private citizen. Here, at Doorn, he spent the last 23 years of his life, living long enough to shake hands with Nazi soldiers, who had trampled over the Netherlands only a few weeks before.

GREAT BRITAIN

In order to consider the monarchy of the British Isles, the history of the nation has been divided into four periods. First, from 959, when Edgar, 'The Pacific', was crowned *King of All England* in Bath Abbey, to 1307. Second, from 1307, when EDWARD II came to the throne as the first Prince of Wales and was accordingly the *King of both England and Wales*, until 1603. Third, JAMES VI of Scotland came to the throne of England on the death of ELIZABETH, the last of the Tudors, so uniting both countries and becoming *King of England, Wales and Scotland*. This position was maintained more or less informally until the the fourth period: the reign of his great-granddaughter, ANNE. During her reign there was an *Act of Union* (May 1, 1707) which officially united the kingdoms of England and Scotland. (There was a further statute of January 1, 1801, which united Great Britain with Ireland, but it seems unnecessarily complicated to dwell on that formality.)

Capital of the kingdom since AD 43 *LONDON*; currency *pound sterling*

ENGLAND

ETHELRED II, 'The Unready' (from *Redeless*: without a council) (968–1016), reigned 978–1016. He came to the throne when his half-brother, Edward, 'The Martyr', was murdered. Ethelred developed the system of paying Danish invaders not to invade, in preference to meeting them in battle. He fled to Normandy in 1013, but was restored to the throne the following year.

EDMUND, 'Ironside' (989–1016), reigned in 1016, being murdered after less than a year on the throne.

CANUTE I (995–1035), reigned 1016–1035. He had already received Mercia, East Anglia and Northumbria by treaty and seized the throne of all England upon EDMUND's death. In 1028 he became CANUTE II of Norway, by right of conquest. One of his first acts was to have the most powerful English chieftains, his potential rivals, put to death.

HAROLD I, 'Harefoot' (1017–1040), reigned 1035–1040. He was the younger of CANUTE's two sons.

HARDICANUTE (1018–1042), reigned 1040–1042. HAROLD's half-brother and King of Denmark from 1035, he was *elected* King of All England.

EDWARD, 'The Confessor' (1004–1066), reigned 1042–1066. Son of ETHELRED, the last Anglo Saxon king, he was also elected by the

Witanagemot (the national assembly of superior churchmen and laymen of the 'upper classes'). He was a saintly man and was canonized by Pope Alexander III in 1161. In 1268, his body was enshrined in Westminster Abbey, the church he founded in 1040.

HAROLD II (1022-1066), reigned in 1066. He was the Earl of Wessex, whose sister had married EDWARD 'The Confessor' in 1045. On October 14, 1066, Harold was killed at the *Battle of Hastings* (in Sussex) – the battle which changed the blueprint of English history.

WILLIAM I, 'The Conqueror' (1025-1087), reigned 1066-1087. He was the bastard son of Robert II, 'The Devil', of Normandy, by his mistress, Harlette. He defeated HAROLD's army in October and was crowned in Westminster Abbey on Christmas Day. It has been written of William that: 'He may worthily take his place as William the Great alongside Alexander and Constantine...'.

WILLIAM II, 'Rufus' (1056-1100), 'The Conqueror's' son, he reigned 1087-1100. William of Malmesbury wrote that at William's court '...the model for young men was to rival women in delicacy of person, to mince their gait, to walk with loose gesture and half naked'. He was killed (probably murdered by William Tirel) in the New Forest and buried without ceremony in Winchester Cathedral.

HENRY I (1068-1135), reigned 1100-1135. By his first wife, Matilda, this fourth son of 'The Conqueror' had a daughter, MATILDA (sometimes called the Empress Maud) who was recognized as heiress presumptive to the English throne in 1119. Matilda was to carry on a civil war against her cousin STEPHEN for a number of years. R.W. Southern said of Henry: 'He contributed nothing to the theory of kingship or to the philosophy of government. He created men'.

STEPHEN (1096-1154), reigned 1135-1154. He was the third son of Adela ('The Conqueror's' sister) by the Count of Blois. At one stage (April to November 1141) MATILDA secured the throne for herself, but was never crowned and eventually renounced her claims entirely. Stephen was the last of the Norman kings.

HENRY II (1133-1189), reigned 1154-1189. The first of the Plantagenets, he was the son of MATILDA and Geoffrey Plantagenet. He married Eleanor of Aquitaine, the divorced wife of LOUIS VII of France. His nickname was 'Curthose' (or 'Curtmantle') as he affected a short 'continental' cloak.

RICHARD I *Coeur de Lion* (1157-1199), the second son of HENRY II, he reigned 1189-1199. Only a few weeks of his reign did he actually spend in his own kingdom. He was either almost permanently crusading, or else a prisoner of Duke Leopold in Austria. He was eventually killed at the siege of Chalus. He married Berengaria of Navarre in 1191, but the union was never consummated.

JOHN, 'Lackland' (1167-1216), reigned 1199-1216. He was RICHARD's younger brother and generally thought of as 'a bad king'. (See, particularly, the *Robin Hood* legend.) John, someone said, was '...the very worst of all our kings, a man whom no oaths could bind, no pressure of conscience, no consideration of policy restrain from evil; a faithless son, a treacherous brother, an ungrateful master; to his people a hated tyrant'. In 1209 he was excommunicated by Pope Innocent III. At Runnymede in June 1215, he did, however, sign the *Magna Carta* for his people.

HENRY III (1206–1272), reigned 1216–1272. A Regency, under Hubert de Burgh, operated until Henry, son of JOHN, was 21, when he declared himself King. His wife, Eleanor of Provence, died as a nun in 1291.

EDWARD I, 'Longshanks' (1239–1307), HENRY's eldest child, reigned 1272–1307. He is buried in Westminster Abbey, despite his wish that his bones were to be carried by his son until the Scottish people had been totally subdued. On his tomb is inscribed *Eduardus primus, Scotorum malleus hic est* – Here is Edward, hammer of the Scots. A great King, who said of himself, 'I should not be a better one however splendidly I was dressed'.

ENGLAND AND WALES

EDWARD II (1284–1327), reigned 1307–1327. In 1301, the fourth son of EDWARD I, was officially made Prince of Wales. He was given to making much of young men, in particular Piers Gaveston. After a troubled reign he was murdered in an obscene manner by Gurney and Maltravers. His murder was commissioned by Lord Berkeley (in whose castle in Gloucestershire the king was prisoner) at the behest of Edward's unscrupulous Queen, Isabella, and her lover, Roger Mortimer.

EDWARD III (1312–1377), reigned 1327–1377. EDWARD II's son, the father of 'The Black Prince', and husband of Philippa of Hainault, he founded the *Order of the Garter*. He was the first king to speak English as his chosen language.

RICHARD II (1366–1399), reigned 1377–1399. He was the son of 'The Black Prince', who had died in 1376. His strife-torn reign ended in his deposition, then murder, in Pontefract Castle, Yorkshire. (Legend had it that he in fact escaped, insane, to France.)

HENRY IV (1366–1413), reigned 1399–1413. With Henry, son of John of Gaunt and usurper of the throne, begins the House of Lancaster. He is the only king to be buried in Canterbury Cathedral.

HENRY V (1397–1422), reigned 1413–1422. The eldest of the usurper's four sons, Henry has been immortalized by Shakespeare. Yet, according to Bowle, he was '…not the bluff patriot of Shakespeare's plays; he was a dour and martial fanatic obsessed by religion and his legal rights'.

HENRY VI (1421–1471), reigned 1422–1471. The son of HENRY V, he became a religious fanatic and most certainly mentally unbalanced. He founded Eton College in 1440. In 1461 he was deposed and treated very shabbily. Nine years later he was restored to the throne for a brief period, only to be deposed a second time, by his cousin, EDWARD. He was murdered whilst at his prayers in the Tower of London.

EDWARD IV (1442–1483), the first king of the House of York reigned 1461–1483. The *Wars of the Roses* the civil war which raged beween the

Yorks and the Lancasters, spelt misery for the country. Edward first seized the throne from HENRY in 1461 and was deposed in 1470, before regaining the throne in 1471. Besides which, during most of his reign England was having trouble with its territorial interests in France.

EDWARD V (1470-1483), son of EDWARD IV, reigned in 1483. He succeeded in April, when his father died, but was placed in the Tower of London for 'safety', on the instructions of his uncle Richard, Duke of Gloucester. His younger (and only surviving) brother, the ten-year-old Richard, was imprisoned with him in the Tower. Neither were seen outside their prison alive. They were probably both suffocated, on June 23, 1483, in the so-called 'Bloody Tower' and the murder was almost certainly countenanced by their uncle.

RICHARD III (1452-1485), reigned 1483-1485. The 'wicked uncle' was reputedly hunch-backed, but was more probably slightly deformed, having been clumsily delivered at birth – a 'breach' baby, possibly. He was killed at the *Battle of Bosworth Field* in his fight with Henry Tudor. During the battle Richard literally lost his crown and his body was probably buried in a common soldier's grave.

HENRY VII (1457-1509), reigned 1485-1509. RICHARD was the last of the Yorks and Henry, the first of the Tudor kings, took the crown of England, but his blood right to the throne must be suspect. He married Elizabeth of York, daughter of EDWARD IV, finally ending the family feuding between the Houses of Lancaster and York. He was shrewd and parsimonious. 'Men feared him, admired him, depended on him, but they did not love him.'

HENRY VIII (1491-1547) reigned 1509-1547. The second son of HENRY VII, Henry took Katherine of Aragon, the widow of his elder brother, Arthur, Prince of Wales (d.1502) as the first of his six wives. In a letter to Erasmus, Lord Mountjoy wrote of the young Henry, upon his accession: 'This king of ours is no seeker after gold, or gems, or mines of silver. He desires only the fame of virtue and eternal life'. Henry was to have five more wives, two of whom he had executed, separate his country from the Church of Rome and still, despite all his faults, set England on its path to glory.

EDWARD VI (1537-1553), reigned 1547-1553. Edward was HENRY's only legitimate son. His mother was Henry's third wife, Queen Jane Seymour, who died two days after the boy's birth at Hampton Court. A sickly boy and 'militant protestant', he died, probably of tuberculosis, before he was sixteen.

LADY JANE GREY (1537-1553), reigned in 1553. She did have some title to the throne, but her supporters' motives were solely selfish or political. She 'reigned' for only nine days. She was beheaded on a February afternoon in the Tower of London, her young husband having been beheaded on Tower Hill that morning.

MARY I (1516-1558), reigned 1553-1558. The rabidly Catholic daughter of HENRY VIII, by Katherine of Aragon, Mary was to marry King PHILIP II of Spain and wage a 'Holy War' against English Protestants.

ELIZABETH I (1533-1603), reigned 1558-1603. MARY's half-sister, she was HENRY VIII's daughter by his second wife, Anne Boleyn. Under Elizabeth, England destroyed the might of Spain's naval power and began to colonize the *New World*. She never married and was the last of the Tudors.

ENGLAND, WALES AND SCOTLAND

JAMES I (1566-1625), reigned 1603-1625. The son of MARY, Queen of Scots, James had been King JAMES VI of Scotland since the age of one. The first Stewart king, he came to the throne of England, because he was the great-great-grandson of HENRY VII, the first of the Tudors. He was a very complex person, fonder of the company of young men than was prudent and saddled with a profligate, Danish wife. He was a passionate huntsman and considered tobacco sinful. At his post-mortem, his head was found to be '...very full of brains'.

CHARLES I (1600-1649), reigned 1625-1649. The second son of JAMES, he was married to Henrietta, daughter of HENRY IV of France. He believed in the 'Divine Right of Kings', fell foul of his Parliament and so precipitated the Civil War. The war began with the *Battle of Edgehill* on October 23, 1642. It ended seven years later with his trial before Parliament, followed by judicial beheading in Whitehall on January 29, 1649.

THE COMMONWEALTH, 1649-1660. A republic was established by Oliver Cromwell, who was made 'Protector', though not until December 1653. All traces of the monarchy were destroyed, even to the extent of removing statues of CHARLES (and replacing at least one of them with an inscription which began, *'Exit Tyrranus Regum Ultimus...'*). Cromwell died in September 1658, aged 59, and was succeeded by his son Richard. He had none of his father's greatness and moves were soon afoot to restore the monarchy. Before long CHARLES's eldest son rode into London in triumph (actually on his thirtieth birthday).

CHARLES II (1630-1685), reigned 1660-1685. 'The Black Boy' or 'Old Rowley' (as he was called amongst other nicknames) was a libertine. The pleasures he took in life were exactly in keeping with the nation's reaction after nearly eleven years of excessively rigorous, Puritanical rule. The king had at least seven official mistresses (by whom he had thirteen illegitimate children, all of whom were supported by Parliamentary allowances and some of whom were given titles which descend to this day). By his mousey little Portuguese wife, Catherine of Braganza, he had no children at all. Pepys recorded of Charles's lady friends that, the 'King doth spend most of his time in feeling them and kissing them naked all over their bodies...but this lechery will never leave him'. Charles, however, was not all sensualist. He had a genuine interest in the Arts and the Sciences and he founded the now internationally prestigious Royal Society. He died a Catholic.

JAMES II (1633-1701), reigned 1685-1688. He was possessed of morals as loose as those of his elder brother CHARLES. According to Pepys he, '...in all things but his *amours* was led by the nose by his wife'. His second wife was the Catholic, Mary of Modena, by whom he was to become the grandfather of 'Bonnie Prince Charlie', the *Young Pretender*. It was his public adoption of catholicism which made him unacceptable to his people and Parliament and led to the so-called *Bloodless Revolution*. He was ousted by his Dutch son-in-law and died an exile in France.

WILLIAM III (1650-1702) and **MARY II,** reigned 1688-1702. William of Orange married Mary, elder daughter of JAMES II (by his first wife) in 1677, when she was 25 years old. They were both devout Protestants and so totally acceptable to the majority of their subjects. They were crowned (uniquely) simultaneously and accorded parallel powers. William, shorter than his wife, was asthmatic and stooped:

> Breathless and faint he moves
> (Or rather stumbles,)
> Silent and dull he sits
> And snorts or grumbles. (Anon)

They had no children and Mary died in 1694. Lonely and unloved, William reigned on for six more years.

UNITED KINGDOM OF GREAT BRITAIN

ANNE (1665-1714), reigned 1702-1714. The corpulent, younger sister of MARY was the last of the Stewarts. By her Danish husband (as fond of the bottle as she) she conceived eighteen children, none of whom survived for long. A few died at birth, some lasted only days. The longest lived was William, Duke of Gloucester, but even he only just saw his eleventh birthday. Macaulay wrote that Anne was, '...when in good humour, meekly stupid and when in a bad humour was sulkily stupid'.

GEORGE I (1660-1727), reigned 1714-1727. He was the first Hanover and King of Great Britain, by virtue of being the great-grandson of JAMES I. (Queen ANNE died on August 1, 1714. Sophia, George's mother, died on June 8. Had she lived 54 days longer, she would have been Queen Sophia of England.) George did little to advance the monarchy; 'a dull, stupid king full of drink and low conversation...'.

GEORGE II (1683-1760), son of GEORGE I, he reigned 1727-1760. The historian Hallam described the period of George's reign as being '...the most prosperous period that England had ever known'. George, 'this strutting Turkey-cock of Herrenhausen', died whilst sitting on a water-closet and was the last king to be buried in Westminster Abbey.

GEORGE III (1738-1820), the grandson of GEORGE II, he reigned 1760-1820. 'In character and convictions he was the average Briton of his day, or what the average Briton aspired to be. He *was* John Bull.' His plain, but fertile wife, Charlotte, presented him with fifteen children over 21 years. (Incredibly, they produced only one legitimate and acceptable heir, even though ten of them married.) George was afflicted by *porphyria* and was declared insane in 1811. His eldest son was made Regent.

GEORGE IV (1762-1830), reigned 1820-1830. This large and brutish man was the eldest son of GEORGE III with whom, in the best Hanoverian tradition, he enjoyed the worst of relationships. In 1785, contrary to the *Royal Marriage Act* of 1772, George married a Catholic, Maria Fitzherbert, a twenty-nine-year-old widow. He was subsequently forced to marry Princess Caroline of Brunswick-Wolfenbüttel (she too was a widow, but one who did not consider cleanliness next to Godliness). He had one daughter by her, Charlotte, who died giving birth to a still-born son in 1817. Charlotte's husband, LEOPOLD, became King of the Belgians in 1831. Lord Aberdeen, one-time Prime Minister, recorded that George was '...certainly a sybarite, but his faults were exaggerated'.

WILLIAM IV (1765-1837), reigned 1830-1837. The younger brother of GEORGE IV, he was amiable, nautical, but not overbright. By his mistress, Mrs Jordan, he had a quiverful of children. Yet, when he eventually married Adelaide of Saxe Meiningen in 1818, he was only able to sire two daughters, both of whom died in infancy.

VICTORIA (1819-1901), reigned 1837-1901. She was the daughter of Edward Duke of Kent, fourth son of GEORGE III, who had been plucked from the arms of his long-standing mistress to marry the widowed Victoria Mary of Saxe-Saalfeld Coburg in 1818. Edward responded to the call and expired from a chill eight months after Victoria was born. On her uncle William's death, little Victoria became Queen of Great Britain, a month after her eighteenth birthday. She was to reign for 64 years and become the head of the largest Empire in the world. She was the last of the Hanovers, but she disliked the thought of her predeceased relations so much, the style of Hanover was not used at her coronation. She married her cousin, Albert of Saxe-Coburg and Gotha, had nine children by him and was desolated when he died from typhoid in 1861, just 42 years old. In November 1858, she was proclaimed in India as the Queen of the 'United Kingdom of Great Britain and Ireland and the colonies and dependencies thereof in Europe, Asia, Africa, America and Australia'. In 1877 she was declared Empress of India itself, in Delhi.

EDWARD VII (1841-1910), reigned 1901-1910. VICTORIA's eldest son, he was the first of the House of Saxe-Coburg and Gotha. He was nearly sixty when he finally eased his not inconsiderable weight onto the throne, having spent the intervening years as a roly-poly play-boy because VICTORIA denied him practically all access to State Papers. He married the beautiful Princess Alexandra of Denmark, of whom he was very fond, though this did not inhibit him from maintaining a number of *petites amoureuses*. He came to be loved by his people and even admired by the French. 'He wasn't clever;' said Admiral, Lord Fisher, 'but he always did the right thing, which is better than brains.'

GEORGE V (1865-1936), reigned 1910-1936. The second son of

EDWARD VII, he inherited his father's lack of intellectual stamina. He had had a naval training and retained a nautical vocabulary. In 1917 he changed the family name from Saxe-Coburg and Gotha to the ultra-British, Windsor. 'Thank God I am an optimist', he once said of himself.

EDWARD VIII (1894-1972), reigned in 1936. Like his namesake and ancestor, EDWARD V, Edward was never crowned. He met, and wished to marry, Wallis Simpson, a twice-divorced American. (She was still married to Ernest Simpson when she first met Edward.) A morganatic marriage was not possible and Edward chose to abdicate rather than create a constitutional crisis, or give up the woman he loved. He was styled as HRH the Duke of Windsor, but his wife, much to his annoyance and her chagrin, was not allowed the dignity of 'Her Royal Highness'.

GEORGE VI (1895-1952), reigned 1936-1952. The second son of GEORGE V, he was happy to remain the Duke of York, until forced onto the throne by the abdication of his brother, EDWARD. He was a retiring man with a pronounced stammer, but his resolution and the support of his wife (née Bowes-Lyon) helped him to overcome the handicap. In the beleaguered and dark days of the Second World War, his kingship was tested and found to triumph. George was the last Emperor of India, the country being granted independence in 1947. He died of cancer at his favourite home, Sandringham House, in Norfolk.

ELIZABETH II (born 1926), her reign began in 1952. The elder of the two daughters of GEORGE VI, she married the ex-Prince Philip of Greece, Philip Mountbatten, who was created Duke of Edinburgh. They have four children; the eldest, Charles, Prince of Wales, being heir to the throne. Elizabeth's reign has seen winds of change blow across monarchies and empires in Europe, but the throne of Great Britain proved itself adaptable.

 # GREECE

After centuries of turbulent history, Greece succeeded in overthrowing the oppressive Ottoman Turkish rule, in a series of bloody skirmishes in the 1820s. The new kingdom, formed in 1829, was recognized by London protocol in 1830.

Capital *ATHENS*; currency *drachma*

OTHO I (1815-1867), reigned 1832-1862. The second son of LUDWIG I of Bavaria, he was chosen to be the King of the Hellenes. He took personal control of the country's government in 1835, when he was only twenty. He was markedly odd and totally Bavarian in outlook. Not surprisingly, he was not popular with his adopted countrymen and fled in the revolution of 1862.

GEORGE I (1845-1913), reigned 1863-1913. The Greeks now changed from the House of Wittelsbach to Oldenburg and elected the son of CHRISTIAN IX of Denmark to their throne. The fact that he was brother-in-law to Edward Albert, Prince of Wales, was not overlooked. In 1867 he married the Russian Grand Duchess Olga and, though his reign was partially successful, it was turbulent and he was assassinated by a Greek called Schinas.

CONSTANTINE I (1868-1923), reigned 1913-1922. The son of GEORGE I, he led the Greek army to victory in the Balkan Wars of 1912-1913. In 1917, he was forced to abdicate by Venizelos (who persuaded the Allies that Constantine was pro-German). He was later re-instated, but finally deposed when Turkey defeated Greece in 1922. When he was 49 years old, an American woman wrote of him, 'he had a childlike appeal which few women can resist'.

ALEXANDER I (1893-1920), reigned 1917-1920. He succeeded his father, when CONSTANTINE was first deposed. Alexander was married to a commoner, by whom he had one daughter. He died from blood poisoning, having been bitten by a pet monkey.

GEORGE II (1890-1947), reigned 1922-1947. Although CONSTANTINE's eldest son, George had been passed over in favour of ALEXANDER, because he was thought to be pro-German (he probably was) in the First World War. He succeeded to the throne after his father's second deposition. After yet another revolution in 1923, George quit Greece, was voted off the throne in 1924, but restored (by plebiscite) in 1935. When the Germans invaded in 1941 he fled to Egypt and then Britain. He was restored to his throne, again by plebiscite, in 1946.

PAUL (1901-1964), GEORGE's younger brother, reigned 1947-1964. He served in the Greek Navy in 1922, went into exile with his brother, in 1924, and then lived in London during the Second World War.

CONSTANTINE II (born 1940), PAUL's son, reigned 1964-1967. He was obliged to leave the country after a coup in 1967. The Greek government allowed him to keep his 80,000 acre (32,300 hectares) estate at Tatoi near Athens, and the family 'home', *Mon Repos*, on Corfu.

HANOVER

The German spelling of this kingdom (which once belonged to the Dukes of Brunswick) has two 'n's, Hannover, and the French call it Hanovre. These, with the English spelling, appeared indiscriminately. It once formed part of Saxony and was raised to a kingdom by the *Treaty of Vienna* in 1814.

Capital *HANNOVER*

GEORGE-WILLIAM-FREDERICK (1738-1820), reigned 1814-1820. He was the country's first king, as the rulers had been styled Electors, since 1692. George-William is much better known as GEORGE III of Great Britain.

GEORGE-AUGUSTUS-FREDERICK (1762-1830), reigned 1820-1830. He was the son of GEORGE, who had been Prince Regent during the last nine years of his father's life and was, of course, GEORGE IV of Great Britain from 1820.

WILLIAM-HENRY (1765-1837), reigned 1830-1837. He was fat GEORGE's brother and King WILLIAM IV of Great Britain.

ERNEST-AUGUSTUS (1771-1851), reigned 1837-1851. The younger brother of GEORGE and WILLIAM, he was also the Duke of Cumberland. Hanover was separated from Britain when William died, making Ernest the first real king of a more or less autonomous country. Unlike his royal brothers, he was tall, once thin, as uncommunicative as they were talkative and an arch conservative. He had been seriously wounded at the Battle of Tournai in 1794, which left his face badly scarred. (Having been damaged, his left eye later went blind and he was probably fitted with an artificial eyeball. His left arm was crippled, too.) In May 1810, the Duke's valet, Sellis, was murdered in St James's Palace – under very strange circumstances. The Duke's thumb was practically severed that night and there were many who thought that he had killed Sellis himself. His wife was the twice-married Princess of Solms-Braunfels. She had jilted his younger brother, the Duke of Cambridge, between her first and second marriages.

GEORGE V (1819-1878), reigned 1851-1866. Cumberland's son and the last King of Hanover. The kingdom was annexed to Prussia in 1866 and George went into exile in Paris. His son, who was to become Queen Alexandra's brother-in-law (Queen Alexandra was the wife of EDWARD VII of Great Britain) was deprived of all British honours because he fought for the German Army in 1919.

HOLY ROMAN EMPIRE

The Empire was never a physical state (or collection of states) in the way other kingdoms discussed in this book are, or were. It was more a state of *mind*. By the end of the eighth century, the Church of Rome realized that the great centralized power it had enjoyed for eight hundred years was declining and admitted the Papacy no longer had the 'muscle' to impose its will, let alone extend it. It needed to add temporal to spiritual strength. In Charlemagne, King of the Franks, it saw a man of personal strength, who ruled a kingdom with material strength which, if allied to the spiritual strength the Church abrogated to itself, could forge the omnipotent union they sought. Accordingly, Charlemagne was invited to fill the newly-created vacancy. On Christmas Day, AD 800, the fifty-eight-year-old king was crowned *Emperor of the Romans* at the Basilica of St Peter in Rome. The theory of Holy Empire, an ecclesiastical theory which embodied actual power, became fact. Fact which lasted over 1000 years. Charlemagne became Charles I and was styled as *Emperor of Romans* which was changed to *Holy Roman Emperor* on the death of Henry, 'The Fowler', in 936. Otto, 'The Great', was the first of the House of Saxony and the first to bear the revised title.

OTTO (980-1002), reigned 983-1002. He was grandson of Otto, 'The Great', and King of Germany.

HENRY II, of Bavaria (973-1024), reigned 1002-1024. The great-grandson of Otto, 'The Great', he was also King of Germany.

CONRAD II, of Franconia (990-1039), reigned 1024-1039. He was the great-great-grandson of Otto, 'The Great', and King of Germany.

HENRY III (1017-1056), reigned 1039-1056. The son of CONRAD, he was also King of Germany.

HENRY IV (1050-1106), reigned 1056-1105. The son of HENRY III and King of Germany, his reign was plagued by Anti-Kings.

RUDOLF (1039-1080), reigned 1077-1080. The son of Kuno, Count of Rheinfelden, Rudolf was the first of a number of challengers to both the throne of Germany and the seat of the Emperor. He married HENRY IV's sister, Matilda, in 1059 and was made administrator of Burgundy. When his brother-in-law was excommunicated by Pope Gregory VII, Rudolf was recognized and crowned at Mainz in March 1077. Constantly engaged in warfare with HENRY's factions, Rudolf finally died from wounds he received in one of these encounters, at Hohenmolsen, in October 1080.

HERMAN (died 1088), reigned 1081-1088. The son of Giselbert of Luxemburg, he was the second of the Anti-Kings. Herman, Count of

Luxemburg, had been elected king by the opponents of HENRY IV. In 1086, Henry was defeated at Wurzburg, but two years later Herman voluntarily withdrew from the power struggle and left the field to Henry. Herman was also Count of Salm, a small county in the Ardennes, between Luxemburg and Liège.

CONRAD, reigned 1093-1098. He was the son of HENRY V by his first wife, Bertha of Savoy and the third Anti-King to emerge in less than fifteen years. He plotted with his father's second wife, the Russian princess, Praxedis (later called Adelaide) and was actually crowned King of Germany in 1087 and King of Italy in 1093, at Monza. He was deposed in 1098.

HENRY V (1081-1125), son of HENRY IV and King of Germany, reigned 1106-1125.

LOTHAIR III, of Supplinburg (1075-1137), reigned 1125-1137. He was an elected King of Germany.

CONRAD III, of Hohenstauffen (1093-1152), reigned 1138-1152. He was a grandson of HENRY IV and King of Germany.

FREDERICK I (1123-1190), Duke of Swabia and King of Germany, he reigned 1152-1190.

HENRY VI (1165-1197), reigned 1190-1197. He was the son of FREDERICK and King of both Germany and Sicily.

PHILIP (1177-1208), reigned 1198-1208. The brother of HENRY VI, he was also King of Germany.

OTTO IV, of Saxony (1174-1218), reigned 1198-1215. Although not an Anti-King, he was 'in competition' with PHILIP. Otto was a grandson of King HENRY II of England, whose daughter, Maud, married Otto's father, Henry, 'The Lion', Duke of Saxony. Otto was probably born at Argenton in France. RICHARD I of England made him Duke of Aquitaine. In 1214, after more than fifteen years of infighting, Otto was defeated at Bouvines and withdrew gracefully to his Brunswick domain.

FREDERICK II, of Sicily (1194-1250), reigned 1212-1250. A son of HENRY VI, Frederick had to cope with two Anti-Kings.

HENRY RASPE, of Thuringia (1202-1247), reigned 1246-1247. An Anti-King, he was the son of Herman of Thuringia and brother of Louis, whose widow, St Elizabeth of Hungary, he expelled in 1227. In April 1246, Pope Innocent (he was hardly that) recommended that Henry Raspe should be elected in place of Frederick. Fortunately, a year later, Raspe expired, leaving a wife but no child, and was the last of the line.

WILLIAM, of Holland (1227-1256), reigned 1247-1256. He succeeded as Count of Holland in about 1234 and was chosen as King of Germany, in opposition to FREDERICK II, and actually crowned in 1248. He was, nevertheless, considered an Anti-King. He died in battle.

CONRAD IV (1218-1254), reigned 1250-1254. The son of FREDERICK II, he was King of Sicily.

RICHARD, of Cornwall (1209-1272), reigned 1257-1272. The second son of King JOHN of England (and brother of HENRY III) Richard was elected Emperor by a very narrow margin. His second wife, Sancha, was the sister of Eleanor, Henry III's wife. Richard took Henry's side in the civil war against Montfort, was captured by the parliamentary forces and held prisoner until Montfort's death in 1265. His own death, in April 1272, was said to have been hastened by the grief occasioned over the murder of his eldest son, Henry of Almain, by Montfort's sons.

ALFONSO X, of Leon and Castile (1221-1284), reigned 1257-1273. Alfonso marked the first appearance of Spanish runners in the Holy Roman race.

RUDOLF, of Habsburg (1218-1291), King of Germany, reigned 1273-1291.

ADOLF, of Nassau (1250-1298), King of Germany, reigned 1292-1298.

ALBERT I (1250-1308), reigned 1298-1308. He was the son of RUDOLF and King of Germany.

HENRY VII (1270-1313), reigned 1308-1313. Apart from being King of Germany, he was also Count Henry of Luxemburg.

LUDWIG, 'The Bavarian', of Upper Bavaria (1286-1347), reigned 1314-1347. He found himself in conflict with the Anti-King, FREDERICK, 'The Fair', of Austria, who was exactly the same age as he.

FREDERICK, 'The Fair' (1286-1330), reigned 1314-1330. Though the second son of ALBERT, he had been denied the Bohemian throne and German crown and made to pay 50,000 marks for Moravia. Frederick considered his treatment very unfair. Despite a majority electing LOUIS king (whom Frederick had beaten in battle) Frederick was crowned at Bonn, thereby beginning a seven-year quarrel. He was imprisoned at Trausnitz from 1322 to 1325.

CHARLES IV, of Luxemburg (1316-1378), another King of Germany, reigned 1346-1378.

GUNTHER, of Schwarzburg (1304-1349), reigned in 1349. The shortest of the Anti-King reigns, he was elected King of Germany on January 30 and died three weeks later. He was a son of Henry, Count of Blankenburg.

VACLAV, of Bohemia (1361-1419), reigned 1378-1400. He was the son of LUDWIG, 'The Bavarian' and King of Germany.

FREDERICK, of Brunswick-Lüneburg (dates unknown), reigned in 1400. He was one of the three grandsons of Magnus of Brunswick (died 1369) who refounded the Wolfenbuttel branch of the House in 1345.

RUPERT III, of the Palatinate (1352-1410), reigned 1400-1410. He was King of Germany and son of the Elector, Rupert II, and Beatrice of Sicily.

JOBST, Margrave of Moravia (1350-1411), reigned 1410-1411. The last of the Anti-Kings, he was nephew of CHARLES IV and grandson of JOHN, 'The Blind', of Bohemia. He was elected in October, a few days after SIGISMUND's election, but died three months later.

SIGISMUND (1368-1437), reigned 1410-1437. He was the King of Germany, Bohemia and Hungary.

ALBERT II, 'The Great' (1397-1439), King of Germany, he reigned 1437-1439.

FREDERICK III, Duke of Austria (1415-1493), reigned 1440-1493. Crowned in Rome in 1452, he was the last Holy Roman Emperor to be so anointed. All his successors automatically became emperors *de facto* on election. He was also King of Germany.

MAXIMILIAN I (1459-1519), reigned 1493-1519. The son of FREDERICK III, he was Archduke of Austria, and King of Germany.

CHARLES V (1500-1556), reigned 1519-1555. He was also CHARLES I of Spain, grandson of MAXIMILIAN and King of Germany.

FERDINAND I (1503-1564), reigned 1558-1564. The brother of CHARLES, Archduke of Austria, He was King of Bohemia and Germany.

MAXIMILIAN II (1527-1576), reigned 1564-1576. He was the son of FERDINAND and King of Germany.

RUDOLF II (1552-1612), the son of MAXIMILIAN and King of Germany, he reigned 1576-1612.

MATTHIAS (1557-1619), reigned 1612-1619. RUDOLPH's brother, he was King of Germany, too.

FERDINAND II, of Styria (1578-1637), reigned 1619-1637. He was the nephew of MAXIMILIAN II and King of Germany and Hungary.

FERDINAND III (1608-1657), reigned 1637-1657. He was the son of FERDINAND II and King of Germany.

LEOPOLD I (1640-1705), reigned 1658-1705. He was FERDINAND III's son and King of Germany.

JOSEPH I (1678-1711) reigned 1705-1711. He was LEOPOLD's son and King of Germany.

CHARLES VI (1685-1740), reigned 1711-1740. JOSEPH's brother and King of Germany, he was 'Pretender' to the Spanish throne.

CHARLES VII (1697-1745), reigned 1742-1745. The son-in-law of JOSEPH I, he succeeded his father, Maximilian Emmanuel, Elector of Bavaria, in 1726. When the *War of Austrian Succession* broke out in 1740, Charles entered into the spirit of the thing and was made King of Bohemia in 1741.

FRANCIS, of Lorraine (1708-1765), reigned 1745-1765. He was the son-in-law of CHARLES VI and Grand Duke of Tuscany. His election was largely due to his wife, MARIE THERESA, who made him co-regent to her not inconsiderable dominions. Francis was quite happy to let the Empress 'look after the shop'. Whilst so doing, she also bore Francis sixteen children, the most famous being Marie Antoinette who, as Queen of France, was to fall victim to the French Revolution.

JOSEPH II (1741-1790), reigned 1765-1790. One of FRANCIS's litter, he was also Archduke of Austria. He co-ruled with his capable mother, becoming sole ruler of the Habsburg domains in 1780. The following year he proclaimed the *Edict of Tolerance* and abolished serfdom.

LEOPOLD II (1747-1792), reigned 1790-1792. He was JOSEPH's brother, MARIE THERESA's third son and Grand Duke of Tuscany from 1765-1790. He formed an alliance with Prussia in February 1792, to take up arms against France. Six months previously his sister, Marie, was taken prisoner by her husband's subjects, who were in revolt. She died only a few days later, before hostilities were joined.

FRANCIS II (1768-1835), reigned 1792-1806. The last Roman Emperor, this son of LEOPOLD II was the first Emperor of Austria. By the time he came to the throne, the Holy Roman Empire was an empty vessel: it was certainly not Holy, neither was it Roman and there was not really an Empire. His own kingdom was widely scattered and vulnerable to attack from a number of directions. In 1806, under NAPOLEON's protection, the Confederation of the Rhine States was formed. Such a substantial, concerted, potential enemy could not be ignored and Francis abdicated from the throne of the Holy Roman Empire. As there was no logical successor, the 'institution' came quietly to an end, after a lifetime of 1006 years.

HUNGARY

The Roman province of Pannonia covered the Hungarian plain south of the Danube. After the Roman retreat, in the fifth century, various barbaric tribes occupied the land until the empire of Attila the Hun was centred here. By the middle of the tenth century the bellicose Magyars had taken over and in 1095 Croatia was included (taking the Hungarian border to the Adriatic). The Arpad family were the rulers until 1301. The Turks came to power 200 years later, but by the end of the seventeenth century the Habsburgs had taken over. This family remained in the ascendant until the Austro-Hungarian Empire was broken up in 1918.

Capital *BUDAPEST*; currency *forint*

STEPHEN (997-1038), reigned 1000-1038. He succeeded as Duke of Hungary, before being crowned, with a royal crown from Pope Silvester, in 1001. He worked hard to convert his people. In 1083, he became the patron saint of the country, when he was canonized, and his remains enshrined. His only son, Emeric, who was killed in a hunting accident, was also revered as a saint.

PETER (1012-1047) reigned 1038-1041. Called Orseolo, the nephew of St STEPHEN, he was deposed in 1041.

ABA (died 1044), reigned 1041-1044. The son-in-law of Duke Geza, father of St STEPHEN (d.997) Aba deposed PETER.

PETER made a short-lived comeback, 1044-1047, before being deposed again, blinded and killed.

ANDREW I (1014–1060), reigned 1047–1060. The great-grandson of Taksony (St STEPHEN's grandfather) he, too, was murdered.

BELA I (1016–1063), reigned 1060–1063. He suppressed the last pagan uprisings and introduced financial reforms. He was killed by a falling tower.

SALOMON (1052–1087), reigned 1063–1074. The son of ANDREW, he was deposed in 1074 by his cousin, GEZA.

GEZA I (died 1077), reigned 1074–1077. BELA's eldest son, he was 'both righteous and generous'.

LADISLAS I (1040–1095), reigned 1077–1095. The brother of GEZA, Ladislas deposed SALOMON, but had to deal with him once more, when he invaded the country with Cuman forces. Ladislas acquired Croatia for Hungary and christianized it. He also introduced a legal code in his enlarged kingdom. Whilst preparing to go on the First Crusade, he died. He was canonized and his relics are enshrined in the cathedral he founded at Nagyvarad.

KOLOMAN (1070–1116), reigned 1095–1116. He was the son of GEZA by a Greek concubine and spent his youth in Poland. He returned to seize the crown when uncle LADISLAS died. In 1113 he imprisoned and blinded his half brother, Almos, the legitimate son of GEZA. Despite this obvious lack of the finer aspects of family feeling, Koloman was reputed to be a wise and farseeing king.

STEPHEN II (1100–1131), reigned 1116–1131. The son of KOLOMAN and known as *Le Foudre* and also *Eclair*.

BELA II (1108–1141), reigned 1131–1141. STEPHEN's nephew, he was blinded by the opposition. His plucky little wife avenged her husband's mutilation by having a few members of the Diet blinded too.

GEZA II (1131–1161), reigned 1141–1161. BELA's son, he spent most of his twenty-year reign at war with his Byzantine cousin, Emperor Manuel Commenus.

STEPHEN III (1148–1172), reigned 1161–1172. The son of GEZA II, he had to contend with his nephews (sons of BELA II) LADISLAS II and STEPHEN IV, who deposed him twice. Anarchy was the order of the day. The younger sprigs were seen off by 1165 and Stephen ruled on, not very happily, for seven more years.

BELA III (1150–1196), reigned 1172–1196. The son of GEZA II, he was brought up in the Byzantine court. After the troubles of his brother STEPHEN's reign, he became 'the most powerful and respected of rulers'. His first father-in-law, the crusader Renaud, had the privilege of being beheaded by Saladin personally. His second wife was sister of PHILIPPE II of France.

EMERIC (1174–1204), reigned 1196–1204. The son of BELA III (by his first wife, the Duchess of Antioch) he was crowned as a baby.

LADISLAS III (died 1205), reigned 1204–1205. He was EMERIC's son. He reigned for only six months and was probably murdered.

ANDREW II (1175–1235), reigned 1205–1235. It is likely he cleared his pathway to the throne by murdering his brother EMERIC's son. He ruined the country's finances and, through weakness, was forced by his nobles to sign *The Golden Bull* of 1222 (Hungary's *Magna Carta*) which gave all lords the right to disallow any royal act.

BELA IV (1206-1270), reigned 1235-1270. He was ANDREW's son, who colonized and christianized Transylvania. He was driven from his country by the Mongol invasion of 1241 and fled to Dalmatia. (Something like half the population of Hungary were killed by the invading armies.) He eventually managed to re-establish himself and finally defeated the Tartar, Nogai Khan, in 1261. Bela had two sons and seven daughters, the most famous being St Margaret of Hungary.

STEPHEN V (1239-1272), reigned 1270-1272. The son of BELA IV, he resisted the invasion of the Bohemian, PREMISLAS. But he was then murdered (probably) upon setting out to find his son, LADISLAS, who had been kidnapped.

LADISLAS IV (1262-1290), reigned 1272-1290. The son of STEPHEN, he lived in a ferment. He ill-treated his wife, Elizabeth of Anjou, and spent the last year of his reign as a fugitive, before being murdered by Cumans in July 1290. (His mother was born a Cuman, the Cumans being an Ugric tribe who invaded Hungary in the late tenth century.)

ANDREW III, 'The Venetian' (1264-1301), reigned 1290-1301. He was the grandson of ANDREW II and the last of the Arpads.

VACLAV (1289-1305), reigned 1301-1305. He was also VACLAV III of Bohemia and Poland, and not considered a real King of Hungary.

OTTO (died 1309), reigned 1305-1309. A descendant of STEPHEN V and Duke of Bavaria, again he was not considered a king

ROBERT, of Anjou (1275-1342), reigned 1309-1342. The great-grandson of STEPHEN V, he was King of Naples and Sicily. He became very attached to Hungary and did much that was good for the country.

LOUIS I, 'The Great' (1326-1382), reigned 1342-1382. In 1370, this son of ROBERT was elected King of Poland.

MARY (1370-1395), reigned 1382-1395. The daughter of LOUIS I, although Queen Regnant, she was called 'King Mary'. She was deposed for a few months, in 1385, by CHARLES III of Naples. Then in February 1387, her husband, SIGISMUND, whom she had married in 1385, joined her as co-ruler.

SIGISMUND (1368-1437), reigned 1395-1437. The King of Bohemia and Holy Roman Emperor, he was not popular in Hungary.

ALBERT (1397-1439), reigned 1437-1439. He was also King of Bohemia and Germany. His father was Albert IV, Duke of Austria and of the House of Habsburg. He spent the two years of his Hungarian reign defending the country against the Turks.

VLADISLAV Jagiellon (1424-1444), reigned 1439-1444. The King of Poland, he was killed by the Turks at the *Battle of Varna*. There followed an interregnum. Later John Hunniades became Regent until 1458.

LADISLAS V (1440-1457), reigned 1444-1457. The son (born posthumously) of ALBERT, he continued to fend off the Turks. He was probably poisoned.

MATTHIAS CORVINUS, 'The Great' (1443-1490), reigned 1458-1490. The son of John Hunniades, Matthias introduced the Renaissance into central Europe. His virtues, his introduction of learning and his sense of justice are better remembered than his despotic attitudes or his introduction of crippling taxation. From 1464 he was also King of Bohemia.

VLADISLAV II (1450-1516), reigned 1490-1516. He was called 'I agree' and elected by the nobles because he could be guaranteed to do so. He was also King of Bohemia.

LOUIS II (1506-1526), reigned 1516-1526. He was the son of VLADISLAV and also King of Bohemia. He was drowned fleeing from the *Battle of Mohács* where the Magyars were completely crushed by the Turks.

JOHN ZAPOLYA (1487-1540), reigned 1526-1540. He was the *Waivode* of Transylvania, elected by the Hungarians and supported (as their puppet) by Turkey.

The next eleven rulers of Hungary, listed below, who reigned 1540-1780, were Archdukes of Austria and Kings of Germany, under which country more details can be found. The dates beside them are dates of accession to the Hungarian throne only and may not, in all cases, be the same date as the rulers' accession to the German throne.

FERDINAND I, 1540
MAXIMILIAN II, 1564
RUDOLPH, 1576
MATTHIAS II, 1608
FERDINAND II, 1618
FERDINAND III, 1637
FERDINAND IV, 1647
LEOPOLD I, 1657
JOSEPH I, 1705
CHARLES III, 1711
MARIA THERESA, 1740

JOSEPH II (1741-1790), reigned 1780-1790. He was the eldest son of MARIA THERESA and Archduke of Austria. He had ruled jointly with his mother since 1765, but not harmoniously. Many of the reforms instituted during their joint reign have been claimed as his, but, in fact, most of the really beneficial ones were originally her ideas. He was married twice: his first wife, Isabella of Parma died in 1763 and his second marriage (a politically arranged misalliance) was very unhappy. There were no children by either union.

LEOPOLD II (1747-1792), reigned 1790-1792. The younger brother of JOSEPH, he had a short and perilous reign. He was troubled by CATHERINE of Russia to the east and France to the west. France, where his sister, Marie Antoinette, was Queen, was in the throes of a revolution.

FRANCIS I (1768-1835), reigned 1792-1835. The son of LEOPOLD, he became Emperor FRANZ I of Austria in 1804. (The Emperor's three successors were also technically kings of Hungary, the last, Charles I, abdicating in 1918.

IRELAND

From about AD 500 until 900, there were a few major 'kingdoms' in Ireland. The modern names for them are Donegal, Londonderry, Armagh and Monaghan, Antrim and Down, Connaught, Munster (which used to be known as *Muma*) Meath and, lastly, Leinster. The occupants of these various 'thrones' are really too numerous to list in a book of this nature. (To afford some idea of the size of the problem: there were 49 High Kings of Tara before BRIAN BORUMA, 67 kings of Cashel and Munster between 450 and 1194, 72 kings of Ulster between 500 and 1201, 68 kings of Leinster between 436 and 1171, 64 kings of Connaught between 450 and 1224, 53 kings of Meath from 466 until 1173, 52 of Ailech from 466 to 1170 and 25 of Dublin from 856 to 1170. There were 401 kings in all!) The review of the Irish monarchy has been restricted to the *Kings of all Ireland* after BRIAN BAROMY (or *Borum* or *Boru*) had forced the 'High King' MAEL SECHMAIL II to submit to him in 1002. In the ninth century AD the Vikings subdued the country and founded small kingdoms centred on Dublin and other parts of the country. Their thrall held until 1014, when they were vanquished by Brian Baromy at Clontarf. The Normans destroyed the resulting Irish kingdoms and from 1170 the island was a *lordship* until becoming attached to the English crown in 1541. A Free State of Ireland was created in 1921 and the country is now known as Eire.

Capital *DUBLIN*; currency *Irish pound*

BRIAN BAROMY, of Munster (926–1014), reigned 1002–1014. During the closing stages of Brian's consolidation, the armies of Dublin and Leinster joined with the Norse Viking army and a battle was fought at Clontarf on Good Friday 1014. Brian gained a decisive victory, but was stabbed in the back (in his tent) by a Viking chief, who had taken refuge in a wood to the rear of the Irish troops.

MAEL SECHMAILL II, of Meath (died 1022), reigned 1014–1022. Subdued by BRIAN in 1002, this king had already reigned for some seventeen years before his overthrow. Confusion, though no lack of kings, followed his demise and the next confirmed monarch was probably BRIAN's grandson.

TURLOUGH O'BRIEN, of Munster (died 1086), reigned 1072–1086. His name was also spelt *Tairrdelbach*. He held court in Limerick.

MURTOUGH O'BRIEN, also spelt *Muirchertach* (died 1114), reigned 1086–1114. The son of TURLOUGH, after him came another spell of comparative kinglessness until DONNELL O'LOUGHLIN.

The apparent inconsistency between the dates of MURTOUGH and DONNELL (below) is caused by a very Irish situation. Several times during this period, either one or other of these 'High Kings' was not accepted by the *majority* of the provinces mentioned in the preamble. Whichever king was out of favour, was referred to as a 'King-in-Opposition'. Even in a book devoted solely to a history of the Irish Monarchy between 1090-1114, the list of their periods of technical sovereignty, would be voluminous.

DONNELL O'LOUGHLIN (died 1121), reigned 1090-1118. The great-great-great-great-great-grandson of a king of Tara, called Aed Findliath, who died in 879.

TURLOUGH O'CONNOR, of Connaught (died 1156), reigned 1118-1156. Pope Adrian IV 'allowed' HENRY II of England to invade Ireland in 1156.

MURTOUGH MACLOUGHLIN, of Ailech (died 1166), reigned 1156-1166. He was DONNELL's grandson.

RORY O'CONNOR, alternatively *Ruaidri Ua Conchobar* (died 1186), the son of TURLOUGH, reigned 1166-1186. In 1177, HENRY II had created his son, JOHN, *Dominus Hibernie* at the Council of Oxford. JOHN visited Ireland in 1185 and under his *Lordship* Ireland was united with the English crown.

ITALY

After the fall of the Roman Empire, a *Scirian Kingdom* centred on Rome lasted until the end of the fifth century. It was followed by the Ostrogoths before the country became part of the Byzantine Empire for a brief period. From 951, the title of King of Italy was used by the Holy Roman Emperor. Before 250 years had passed, the country had been divided into a number of small states, such as; Guastalla, Modena, the Duchy of Milan and so on. Napoleonic Italy began to have a political meaning, but the country was only truly unified in 1860, under the House of Savoy.

The capital was declared to be *ROME* in 1871; currency *lira*

VICTOR EMANUEL II (1820-1878), reigned 1861-1878. Called the 'Honest King', he was the son of CHARLES-ALBERT of Sardinia and had been King of Sardinia since 1849. He encouraged Garibaldi in his efforts to dislodge the Bourbons and openly encouraged the Duchies to rebel.

UMBERTO I (1844-1900), reigned 1878-1900. VICTOR's eldest son, he was assassinated at Monza by an anarchist, called Bresci. An attempt to murder this good-humoured man, had already been made near Rome, by a thug called Acciarito, in April 1897.

VICTOR EMANUEL III (1869-1947), reigned 1900-1946. He and his advisers completely failed to appreciate the threat that Mussolini and his Fascists posed to the monarchy. Twenty-five years later, with Mussolini dead and Allied Armies driving German Nazi troops north through his country, Victor Emanuel misjudged events again. He abdicated too late to give the Italian monarchy even the remotest chance to make a comeback in defeated Italy.

UMBERTO II (born 1904), reigned in 1946. His father, VICTOR EMANUEL III, abdicated on May 9, 1946 and on June 13 a national referendum clearly showed that the Italian people wanted no more kings. Umberto (and his descendants) were barred from Italy forever. He did not, however, abdicate.

LEON
AND ASTURIAS

Leon, an ancient north-western Spanish city, derives its name from the *Legio Septima Gemina* of Galba, stationed here by the later Roman Emperors. It capitulated to the Moors in 717 and became a Spanish kingdom under Garcia, in about 910.

ALFONSO (994-1028), reigned 999-1028. He attempted to spread Christianity throughout his kingdom and died whilst besieging the Mohameddans in Northern Portugal.

VERMUDO III (1016-1037), reigned 1028-1037. Son of ALFONSO and brother-in-law of FERDINAND of Castile who killed him in battle at Tamaron.

LEON
AND CASTILE

(★ indicates King of Castile only.)

FERDINAND I, *El Magno* (died 1065), reigned 1035-1065. The son of SANCHO III of Navarre, he became King, by conquest, of Leon and Asturias in 1037. In 1056 he declared himself 'Emperor of Spain', having disposed of his cousin Garcia in 1054.

SANCHO II★, 'The Strong' (1038-1072), reigned 1065-1072. The son of FERDINAND, he was assassinated.

ALFONSO, *El Bravo* (1040-1109), reigned 1072-1109. SANCHO II's brother, he became a sort of 'hero of the people', as a result of his resistance to Moorish invasion.

URRACA (1080-1126), reigned 1109-1126. She was the daughter of ALFONSO, 'The Brave', and divorced from ALFONSO, of Aragon, with whom she was at loggerheads. She did not see eye to eye with their son either.

ALFONSO VII (1104-1157), reigned 1126-1157. Despite the war waged with his mother, URRACA, Alfonso happily took her throne and nine years later announced himself as Emperor of Spain.

SANCHO III★, 'The Beloved' (1134-1158), reigned 1157-1158. ALFONSO's son, he married Blanca of Navarre.

ALFONSO VIII★ (1155-1214), reigned 1158-1188. He was King of Castile alone, because Leon was separated from it in 1157, under FERDINAND II. He married Eleanor, daughter of HENRY II of England, and founded the university of Palencia in 1209 – the first of the Spanish universities.

FERDINAND II (1145-1888), King of Leon 1157-1188. ALFONSO VIII's brother, he defeated his father-in-law, ALFONSO I of Portugal, at Badajoz in 1167 and took him prisoner.

ALFONSO IX (1166-1230), reigned 1188-1230. He was FERDINAND's son. The Pope declared both his marriages invalid for being 'within the degrees of affinity'. Well might the Pope be worried: Alfonso was called 'The Slobberer' and used to foam at the mouth.

HENRY I★ (1203-1217), reigned 1214-1217. The son of ALFONSO VIII and, like his father, King of Castile.

FERDINAND III★ (1200-1252), reigned 1217-1252. He was canonized by Clement X in 1671, but on what grounds it is hard to imagine. He captured Cordoba and Seville from the Moors and, under him, Leon was permanently united with Castile. He married the daughter of ALFONSO VIII.

ALFONSO X, 'The Wise' (1221-1284), reigned 1252-1282. The son of FERDINAND III, he was also known as 'The Astronomer'. Under his control the *Alphonsine Tables* were drawn up. He had the Bible translated into Castilian and so created the national language. Although never crowned, he was elected Holy Roman Emperor. He was unseated by his second son.

SANCHO IV (1258-1295), reigned 1282-1295. He was called 'The Great and the Brave', because he conquered the Moors at Jarifa. Having usurped his father's throne, he was troubled by the claims of the true king, his nephew.

FERDINAND IV, 'The Summoned' (born 1285), reigned 1295-1312. He was the son of SANCHO IV.

ALFONSO XI (1311-1350), reigned 1312-1350. The son of FERDINAND IV, he was a ferocious man sometimes known as 'The Avenger'. He dispensed justice arbitrarily, neglected his Portuguese wife and had a large, publicly acknowledged, illegitimate brood by his mistress Leonora. It was the Black Death that eventually killed him.

PEDRO, 'The Cruel' (1334-1369), reigned 1350-1366 and again from

1367-1369. With the help of 'The Black Prince' (the Prince of Wales, son of EDWARD III of England) Pedro defeated his illegitimate brother, Henry, and deposed him at Najera in 1367. Two years later the tables were turned and Henry took Pedro prisoner at Montiel and put him to death.

HENRY II (1333-1379), reigned 1366-1367 and again from 1369-1379. The illegitimate son of ALFONSO XI, he seized PEDRO's throne, but occupied it only until the *Battle of Najera* a year later. In 1369 he returned to the fray and had PEDRO murdered. Ten years later he was poisoned by a monk. Henry was probably crueller than 'The Cruel', Pedro, yet he was nicknamed 'The Gracious'.

JOHN I (1358-1390), reigned 1379-1390. The son of HENRY II, he united Biscay with Castile.

HENRY III (1379-1406), reigned 1390-1406. The poorly son of JOHN, he was called 'The Sufferer'.

JOHN II (1405-1454), reigned 1406-1454. He was the son of HENRY III.

HENRY IV (1425-1474), reigned 1454-1474. The son of JOHN, '...weak and vacillating in character...his reign was marked by incidents of the most ignominious kind'. He was nicknamed 'The Impotent' and there was not a little speculation as to whether the daughter produced by Joan of Portugal, his wife, was (or could have been) his.

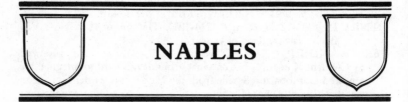

NAPLES

Naples was once part of ROGER II's Kingdom of Sicily. When the Anjous were evicted from Sicily, after the *Sicilian Vespers* in 1282, they kept Naples for themselves. From December 1816, both Naples and Sicily were absorbed into the Kingdom of Italy.

ROGER (1093-1154), reigned 1130-1154. Having been King of Sicily for a year, he became King of Naples. The nine kings who followed him, down to CHARLES of Anjou, were all Kings of Sicily (see Sicily).

CHARLES II (1245-1309), reigned 1285-1309. He was the son of CHARLES of Anjou and called 'The Lame', possibly as a result of a childhood injury.

ROBERT, 'The Wise' (1275-1343), reigned 1309-1343. The son of CHARLES II, he unwisely tried to recover his grandfather's Sicilian throne.

JOANNA I (1326-1382), reigned 1343-1382. She was ROBERT's granddaughter. Since a handy divorce was not easily available, Joanna arranged for the disposal of her first husband, Prince Andrew of Hungary. For this she was expelled by LOUIS of Hungary, in 1345. A year later she married Louis of Taranto. Her bothersome reign ended with her death by suffocation, at the hands of her successor.

CHARLES III (1345-1386), reigned 1382-1386. Charles was of the Durazzo branch of the House of Anjou and also King of Hungary. He was murdered in Buda.

LADISLAS (1377-1414), reigned 1386-1414. The son of CHARLES III, he tried to unite all Italy. He only succeeded in expelling Pope John XXIII in 1413. (John was, in fact, an *Anti-Pope*).

JOANNA II (1371-1435), reigned 1414-1435. She was LADISLAS's sister. When she died, she bequeathed her crown to Regnier, of Anjou, who was then twenty-six. He reigned in name only until eventually ALFONSO, of Aragon, took over the kingdom which Joanna had left him in her will. Regnier never relinquished his claim to the throne.

ALFONSO I, 'The Wise' (1385-1458), reigned 1442-1458. From 1416 he was also ALFONSO V of Aragon.

FERDINAND I (1424-1494), reigned 1458-1494. He was ALFONSO's illegitimate son. Not only was he kept busy by a barons' revolt, but Regnier continued to press his claims.

ALFONSO II (1448-1495), reigned 1494-1495. He was the son of FERDINAND and Isabella. Having made himself totally obnoxious, he abdicated when the French invaded in January 1495.

FERDINAND II (1469-1496), reigned 1495-1496. The son of ALFONSO II, he drove out the French, helped not a little by FERDINAND of Castile's General de Cordova, and recovered his kingdom.

FREDERICK IV (1452-1504), reigned 1496-1501. The son of FERDINAND I, he was deposed after an invasion of French and Aragonese troops. There followed an interregnum, while France and Aragon discussed the future of Naples. After two years, Spain became master of the kingdom and remained so until the advent of the House of Savoy in 1713.

VICTOR-AMADEUS (1666-1732), reigned 1713-1718. He was King of Sardinia and had received the island of Sicily under the *Treaty of Utrecht* but was obliged to hand it back to Spain. In 1734, the *Treaty of the Escurial* between France, Spain and Savoy (against Austria) was signed and CHARLES III of Spain became king.

CHARLES IV (1716-1788), reigned 1734-1759. In 1738 he was recognized as King of the Two Sicilies and Spain renounced all claim. He succeeded to the Spanish crown in 1759 and abdicated in favour of his son.

FERDINAND I (1751-1825), reigned 1759-1806. CHARLES's son, he was born in Naples, fled the kingdom in 1806 and ruled over Sicily alone until 1815. In 1815 he returned to Naples (see after JOACHIM MURAT).

JOSEPH BONAPARTE (1768-1844), reigned 1806-1808. The elder brother of NAPOLEON, he was a trained lawyer whom the Emperor sent to Naples to expel the Bourbons. He set about trying to tackle the mountainous fiscal problems of the Neapolitans and stayed there for two years. All the while he fended off British attacks, until his brother 'posted' him to Spain in May 1808.

JOACHIM MURAT (1771-1815), he reigned 1808-1815. A French general, he was Marshal of France and NAPOLEON's brother-in-law. With his 'black hair flowing in curls over his shoulders: his hat gorgeous with plumes: his whole dress carrying an air of masquerade', this lascivious innkeeper's son cut a conspicuous figure. He had been more than helpful in the 1799 *coup d'état*. Napoleon, however, found him a little too zealous on the throne of Naples. When his brother-in-law fell, Murat behaved true to form and deserted the French cause, hastily turning his coat again during the 'Hundred Days'. He was finally captured and shot in Calabria.

FERDINAND I, reigned 1815-1825. Now 64 years old, he was none other than the Ferdinand who first came to the throne before the Bonapartists in 1759. Once again he reconsolidated Sicily and Naples. From 1825-1861 FERDINAND's grandson and great-grandson ruled (details of whom may be found under the *Two Sicilies*). On September 7, 1860, Garibaldi entered Naples to a rapturous welcome and a plebiscite finally amply demonstrated the desire to dismantle the Kingdom of Naples. It became part of VICTOR EMANUEL's Italy in 1861.

 # NAVARRE

In the eleventh century, SANCHO, 'The Great', began to rule a region of northern Spain which had been a kingdom since the Mohammedan conquest of the Visigoths. Sancho created Leon and Castile, leaving Navarre out on its own. Relatively undeveloped, it was taken over by the Counts of Champagne, until practically all of it was drawn into Spain in 1516. Today Navarre is a province of Spain.

Capital *PAMPLONA*

SANCHO III (992-1035), reigned 1000-1035. A king of Pamplona who, having pushed back the Moors, proclaimed himself Emperor. He then weakened his rule by dividing his kingdom.

GARCIA IV (died 1054), SANCHO's son reigned 1035-1054.

SANCHO IV (born 1038), reigned 1054-1076. The son of GARCIA, he was deposed by the 'Aragon branch'. The date of his death is unknown.

SANCHO V (1037-1094), the nephew of Garcia III, reigned 1076-1094.

PEDRO (1068-1104), son of SANCHO V, reigned 1094-1104.

ALFONSO (died 1134), reigned 1104-1134. He was the brother of PEDRO and ALFONSO I of Aragon.

GARCIA V (died 1150), reigned 1134-1150. The first of the House of Navarre, he was chosen by the nobles of the country.

SANCHO VI, 'The Wise', reigned 1150-1194. He (wisely) chose to be styled as King of Navarre rather than Pamplona.

SANCHO VII, 'The Strong' (died 1234), reigned 1194-1234. He was both a dashing Spaniard and the last full-blooded one to be King of Navarre. His various successors were more Gallic than Iberian.

THEOBALD I, 'The Posthumous', of Champagne (1201-1253), reigned 1234-1253. He was a nephew of SANCHO VII by Sancho's sister. Later he married Sancho's daughter who would have been his first cousin – yet the marriage was not banned.

THEOBALD II (1207-1270), reigned 1253-1270. He was the son of THEOBALD I, by his marriage to his uncle's daughter.

HENRY I (1210-1274), reigned 1270-1274. THEOBALD II's brother, he was called Henry 'Crassus'.

JOANNA I (1273-1305), HENRY's daughter reigned 1274-1305. She married PHILIPPE IV of France, so Navarre passed to the French and Philippe became FELIPE I of Navarre until he died in 1314.

LOUIS I (born 1289), reigned 1314-1316. He was also LOUIS X, *Le Hutin* of France, son of JOANNA and Felipe.

PHILIPPE II (1293-1322), reigned 1316-1322. He was LOUIS's brother and PHILIPPE, 'The Tall', King of France.

CHARLES I (1294-1328), reigned 1322-1328. Also CHARLES IV of France, he was the brother of LOUIS and PHILIPPE and the last of the Capets.

JOANNA II (1311-1349), reigned 1328-1349. The daughter of LOUIS X of France, she ruled with her husband, Philip of Evreux. Under them, Navarre became an independent kingdom once again.

CHARLES II (1332-1387), reigned 1349-1387. He was known, deservedly, as 'The Bad'. Forever untrustworthy, Charles, finding an ally in England, tried to enlarge his kingdom, but du Guesclin put an end to that in 1364.

CHARLES III, 'The Noble' (born 1361), reigned 1387-1425. Although a contrast to his father, 'The Bad', he was not really very noble.

BLANCHE (1405-1441), reigned 1425-1441. The daughter of CHARLES III, she ruled with her husband, JOHN.

JOHN, of Aragon (1397-1479), reigned 1441-1479. BLANCHE's second husband, he ruled alone after her death.

ELEANOR (died 1479), reigned in 1479. The daughter of JOHN and BLANCHE, she was the last of the House of Trastamara.

FRANCIS-PHOEBUS, of Foix, ELEANOR's grandson, reigned 1479-1483.

CATHERINE (died 1512), reigned 1483-1512. The sister of FRANCIS-PHOEBUS, she ruled for one year alone and then together with her husband, JOHN Albret.

JOHN III (died 1516), CATHERINE's widower, reigned 1512-1516.

During his reign, Aragon seized the Spanish portion of the country, leaving a small Basque 'kingdom' nestling in the Pyrenees.

HENRI II (1503–1555), reigned 1516–1555. The son of CATHERINE and JOHN, he was a man of taste and culture.

JOANNA (1528–1572), reigned 1555–1572. HENRY's daughter and a devout Huguenot, she ruled with her husband, Anthony de Bourbon, who died in 1562. Her religious beliefs led her to become involved in the religious wars being fought in France. Their son became HENRY IV of France in 1589.

THE NETHERLANDS

The Netherlands is the correct name for the country of which Holland is part. In medieval times the country was divided into states (the county of Holland being the most important). Most of them eventually passed to Burgundy, then to the Austro-Spanish Empire, until the people of the Netherlands revolted against PHILIP II. In 1579 the United Provinces came into being. This lasted until 1795, when the French invaded and established the Batavian Republic, which became the Kingdom of Holland under Napoleon.

Capital *AMSTERDAM* but the seat of government is at The Hague; currency *gulden*

LOUIS BONAPARTE (1778–1846), reigned 1806–1810. One of NAPOLEON's numerous brothers, he was made King of Holland not long after the splendid French victory at Austerlitz. Napoleon meant his brother to be little more than a puppet king, but Louis took the job more than seriously. He tried to prevent the Emperor from annexing Holland (to stop trade with the hated English) but Napoleon invaded the Dutch capital. Louis fled, having abdicated, and on July 9 1810, Holland was annexed. Louis settled in Rome and watched the progress of his sons with some pride. His youngest son, Louis (by the lovely Hortense de Beauharnais, daughter, by her first marriage, of Napoleon's second wife, Josephine) became the Emperor NAPOLEON III in 1852.

NAPOLEON-LOUIS BONAPARTE (born 1804), reigned in 1810, for all of five days, after his father fled before his uncle's invading army.

WILLIAM I (1772–1844), reigned 1815–1840. The son of the dismissed *Stadtholder* (William V, who died in 1806) William was in command of the army beaten by NAPOLEON's French army in 1810. The House of Orange was restored in 1813, with William as *Stadtholder*. He was promoted to king after the extinction of the Napoleonic Empire. William married a Belgian Catholic and this religious miscegenation so offended the low church lowlanders, that he felt he had to abdicate. He retired to Silesia for the last four years of his life.

WILLIAM II (1792-1849), reigned 1840-1849. The son of WILLIAM I, he served under Wellington in the *Peninsular War* in Spain. He had a liberal outlook, instigated many reforms and granted the country a democratic constitution.

WILLIAM III (1817-1890), reigned 1849-1890. He continued his father's reformation, creating more liberal conditions.

WILHELMINA (1880-1960), reigned 1890-1948. She was the daugher of WILLIAM III and his second wife, Emma. At one time she was reputed to be the 'richest woman in the world', she was certainly one of the plainest. She abdicated in favour of her daughter.

JULIANA (born 1909), reigned 1948-1980. She eventually inherited much of her mother's wealth, as well as her kingdom. In 1930, before her marriage, which produced four daughters, she graduated with a law degree from Leyden University.

BEATRIX (born 1938), her reign began in 1980. She is the eldest daughter of JULIANA, who abdicated in her favour when she came of age. Beatrix married Claus van Amsberg, a German. Not a diplomatic choice, perhaps, in the light of the German occupation of her country from 1940 to 1944.

NORWAY

In the ninth century, Harald, 'The Fairhair', *Jarl* of Westfold, became king of a more or less united country. Despite much fighting and squabbling, his descendants ruled until 1319. Then in 1387, MARGARET of Denmark became Queen. The two countries were joined by having a common sovereign for 400 years. This lasted until 1814, when Sweden took the country over. By 1905, independence had been negotiated and the Oldenburgs were back on the throne.

Capital *OSLO*; currency *krone*

OLAF I, of the Tryggvesson family (965-1000), reigned 995-1000. Great-grandson of Harald, 'The Fairhair', his father Trygve was murdered and his mother, Astrid, expelled. Educated in Russia, Olaf became a Viking. He put himself on the throne at the end of a twenty-five-year interregnum, following the death of Harald II in 970. He was killed, probably drowned, in a naval battle against his own disaffected *jarls* fighting with the Swedes and the Danes. There followed a fifteen-year interregnum.

OLAF II, St Olaf (995–1030), reigned 1015–1028. As a teenager he was fighting for King ETHELRED in England against the Danes. He returned a Christian. Though canonized he spread the gospel in a very unsaintlike manner, using both bribery and strongarm tactics. All this caused such unpopularity, he was driven from the country by the Anglo Danish CANUTE. In trying to get back to power, he was killed at the *Battle of Stiklestad* on the Trondheim fjord. Rather confusingly he is patron saint of Norway and enshrined in the Cathedral of Nidaros.

CANUTE, King of England (1016–1035), reigned 1028–1035.

MAGNUS I, 'The Good' (1024–1047), reigned 1035–1047. St OLAF's son, he ruled alone until 1046, when he ruled jointly with HARALD III for a year, before being killed in battle.

HARALD III, *Hardrada* (meaning a stern man in council) (1015–1066), reigned 1047–1066. He was sole ruler from 1047, having shared the throne since the age of twenty. He was killed by HAROLD II of England at the *Battle of Stamford Bridge*.

MAGNUS II (1048–1069), reigned 1066–1069. The son of HARALD III, he was co-ruler with OLAF III.

OLAF III (1050–1093), reigned 1066–1093. He was called *Kyrre* meaning man of peace. He ruled with his brother MAGNUS II.

MAGNUS III, 'The Barefoot' (1073–1103), reigned 1093–1103. The son of OLAF III, he ended up another battle casualty.

OLAF MAGNUSSON (1091–1115), reigned 1103–1115. He was the son of MAGNUS III and co-ruler with his two brothers.

EYESTEIN I (1089–1122), reigned 1103–1122. He ruled in fraternal concord with OLAF MAGNUSSON and SIGURD I.

SIGURD I (1090–1130), reigned 1103–1130. The longest ruling of the happy band of brothers. He was the first Norwegian king to go on a Crusade.

MAGNUS IV (1115–1139), reigned 1130–1135. SIGURD's son, he ruled with HARALD IV (who could have been his illegitimate half-brother) until he was blinded and deposed. He eventually died in battle.

HARALD IV (1103–1136), reigned 1135–1136. He claimed to be the bastard son of MAGNUS III, but at this distance it seems doubtful.

SIGURD II (born 1134), the son of HARALD IV, reigned 1136–1155.

INGE I, 'The Hunchback' (1135–1161), reigned 1136–1161. He ruled with his half-brother, SIGURD, until 1155, and then alone until he was killed in 1161.

EYESTEIN II (1125–1157), reigned 1142–1157. He was possibly a brother of the last two, but he claimed to be a by-blow of HARALD IV's. Not really to be counted.

HAAKON II (born 1147), reigned 1161–1162. The son of SIGURD, he was co-ruler with MAGNUS V.

MAGNUS V, Erlingsson (1156–1184), reigned 1161–1184. Co-ruler with HAAKON II, he was a grandson, through female descent, of SIGURD I. He was killed in battle by a cousin called SVERRE.

SVERRE, Sigurdsson (1152–1202), reigned 1184–1202. He was possibly a son of SIGURD II. A priest from the Faroes, he sufficiently forgot his calling to kill poor young MAGNUS. He did, however, start to restore order. Part of his campaign was to bridle the power of the bishops. He was so successful at this that they complained to Rome and Sverre was excommunicated.

HAAKON III, Sverresson (1177–1204), reigned 1202–1204. His short reign ended when he was poisoned by his stepmother, SVERRE's second wife.

INGE II, Baardsson (1195–1217), reigned 1204–1217. He was a grandson of SIGURD II and a nephew of SVERRE.

HAAKON IV, 'The Old' (1204–1263), reigned 1217–1263. He was the son of HAAKON III, who died before the boy was born. The baby was placed in the care of INGE. He ruled well, ended the civil war and established Norway as a commercial and maritime power of consequence.

MAGNUS VI, 'The Law Mender' (1238–1280), reigned 1263–1280. He was the son of HAAKON IV.

ERIK II, Magnusson (1268–1299), the son of MAGNUS VI, reigned 1280–1299.

HAAKON V (1270–1319), reigned 1299–1319. He was ERIK II's brother. His commercial policies in relation to the *Hanseatic League* had damaging long-term effects on Norwegian trade.

MAGNUS VII (1316–1374), reigned 1319–1355. The grandson, on his mother's side, of HAAKON V, he was also MAGNUS IV of Sweden.

HAAKON VI, Magnusson (1340–1380), reigned 1343–1380. He was co-ruler with his father, MAGNUS VII, from 1343–1345 and King of Sweden from 1362.

OLAF IV (died 1387), reigned 1380–1387. He was HAAKON VI's son and OLAF V of Denmark.

MARGARET (1352–1412), reigned 1387–1412. The mother of OLAF IV, she was also Queen of Denmark.

From 1412 until 1814, the Kings of Denmark were also Kings of Norway. For the record, they are listed below, with the dates of accession only beside them. Further details can be found under Denmark.

ERIK VII, 1412
(Interregnum 1438)
CHRISTOPHER III, 1440
CHRISTIAN I, 1448
JOHN, 1481
CHRISTIAN II, 1513
FREDERICK I, 1523
CHRISTIAN III, 1533
FREDERICK II, 1559
CHRISTIAN IV, 1588
FREDERICK III, 1648
CHRISTIAN V, 1670

FREDERICK IV, 1699
CHRISTIAN VI, 1730
FREDERICK V, 1746
CHRISTIAN VII, 1766

FREDERICK VI, 1808. Frederick continued to reign in Denmark until 1836, but in 1814 Norway was united in a *Personal Union* with Sweden and the next five Kings were also Kings of Sweden. Fuller details of these will be found under Sweden.

CHARLES I, 1814
CHARLES II, 1818
OSCAR I, 1844
CHARLES III, 1859

OSCAR II, 1872. Oscar renounced the Norwegian throne on June 7, 1905 and the Oldenburg line was reintroduced to Norway.

HAAKON VII (1872–1951), reigned 1905–1951. He was the second son of FREDERICK VIII, of Denmark, and the first elected king. He did not accept the crown until a Norwegian plebiscite had been held and the people themselves had shown him to be 'suitable'. He was crowned at Trondheim in June. In July 1896, he had married the twenty-seven-year-old Princess Maud, daughter of King EDWARD VII of England (and his cousin). His genuine simplicity endeared him to his new subjects and their loyalty was strengthened by his demeanour, while exiled from Norway, during the Second World War.

OLAF V (born 1903), whose reign began in 1951. The only son of HAAKON and Maud, he was born at Sandringham House, the home of his English grandfather, and christened Alexander. It was not until 1905 (when his father became King of Norway and changed his name to Haakon) that he was called Prince Olaf. He is a fine yachtsman, a first class skier and a great Anglophile.

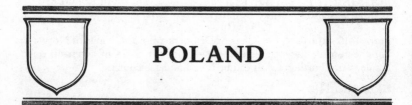

POLAND

A dynasty, established by the legendary Piast, ruled Poland in the tenth century. It was a major power in Eastern Europe. By the first quarter of the fourteenth century, a new kingdom had been created. In 1370 the throne passed to the Angevins then to a Lithuanian dynasty, who formed an immense country; an all-powerful state, holding sway until the end of the Jagiellons in 1572. Under the Vasas the crown was elective and powerful, but was declining by the eighteenth century. In 1795 the great area was split up between Austria, Russia and Prussia. NAPOLEON established a Grand Duchy, which Russia overran in 1813. As the Russian

Tsars called themselves Kings of Poland, a truly independent country did not emerge until 1918. It was partitioned again in 1939, between Nazi Germany and Russia. The final 'surgery' took place in December 1948, when Russia effectively took control. The republic was given a new constitution in July 1952, which was finally modified in February 1976.

Capital *WARSAW*; currency *zloty*

BOLESLAV I, 'The Brave' (966–1025), reigned 992–1025. He had been Duke of Great Poland from his accession until he was declared 'king' in 1024. He was the son of Mieszko, Prince of Poland.

MIESZKO II (990–1034), reigned 1025–1034. He was BOLESLAV's brother. In 1031 another brother. Bezrin, appeared on the scene for a year or so.

KASIMIR I (born 1016), reigned 1034–1058. He was called 'The Restorer', 'The Peaceful' or even 'The Monk'. In 1037 he was deposed. Two years later he was restored and rebuilt the country, mostly on a Christian base.

BOLESLAV II, 'The Intrepid' (1039–1079), reigned 1058–1079. KASIMIR's son, he was finally excommunicated and fled the country with his sons. He died in Hungary.

VLADISLAV I, 'The Careless' (1043–1102), reigned 1079–1102. The son of KASIMIR, he abdicated and died in the same year.

BOLESLAV III, 'Wrymouth' (1085–1138), reigned 1102–1138. He was the son of VLADISLAV. He waged war unsuccessfully against Hungary and Bohemia.

VLADISLAV II, 'The Exile' (1104–1159), reigned 1138–1145. He was deposed by his brothers, all sons of BOLESLAV.

BOLESLAV IV, 'Curly' (1127–1173), reigned 1146–1173. Deposed, like his brother VLADISLAV, he died within months.

MIESZKO III, 'The Old' (1126–1202), reigned 1173–1177. The last of the brothers and, in turn, also deposed. He returned to the throne from 1198 to 1202.

KASIMIR II, 'The Just' (1138–1194), reigned 1177–1194. He introduced laws which protected the peasantry from the nobles.

LESZEK I, 'The White', of Mazoria (1185–1227), reigned 1194–1198. KASIMIR's son, he was deposed, but returned 1202–1227.

BOLESLAV V (1221–1279), reigned 1227–1279. He was LESZEK's son and called 'The Chaste'.

LESZEK II, 'The Black' (died 1289), reigned 1279–1289. He was the Duke of Sieradz and great-grandson of KASIMIR II.

VLADISLAV (born 1260), reigned 1289–1290. He was deposed in 1290, restored in 1306 and made king in 1320 (see below).

PRZEMISLAV (died 1296), reigned 1290–1296. He was Duke until 1295, when he was made king, but assassinated soon afterwards.

VACLAV I (1271–1305), reigned 1296–1305. The son-in-law of PRZEMISLAV, he was also VACLAV II, King of Bohemia.

VACLAV II (1289–1306), reigned 1305–1306. The son of VACLAV I, he was VACLAV III of Bohemia.

VLADISLAV I (see above), reigned 1306–1333. He was finally made

King of Poland on January 20, 1320, when, for some reason, the Vladislavs were renumbered. He strengthened his country and made effective political marriages for his children.

KASIMIR III, 'The Great' (1310-1370), reigned 1333-1370. Diplomatically, culturally and judicially, he was a great man. He befriended the Jews and built extensively; '...he found a country of wood and left a country of stone'.

LOUIS (1326-1382), reigned 1370-1382. The son of KASIMIR's sister, Elizabeth, he was also King LOUIS of Hungary. A two-year interregnum followed his reign.

JADWIGA (1373-1399), reigned 1384-1399. LOUIS's daughter, she married VLADISLAV, who ruled with her from 1386. He was Duke of Lithuania. Her *election* to the throne (being a younger daughter) set a pattern for an elective monarchy in the future.

VLADISLAV II (1350-1434), reigned 1386-1434. He continued to rule alone after JADWIGA's death and was the first of the Jagiellon dynasty. He brought Lithuania into the kingdom, so Poland now had the Baltic on the west and stretched as far as the Ukraine in the east.

VLADISLAV III (1424-1444), reigned 1434-1444. He was also King VLADISLAV of Hungary. Killed in battle, a three-year interregnum followed his rule.

KASIMIR IV (1427-1492), reigned 1447-1492. VLADISLAV's brother, he acquired large land holdings in Bohemia, Silesia and Hungary, and drove the Turks out of Moldavia.

JOHN I, Albert (1459-1501), reigned 1492-1501. He was the fourth son of KASIMIR and elected to the throne.

ALEXANDER Jagiellon (1461-1506), reigned 1501-1506. An impoverished reign, funds were lacking to support an army and Russians roamed Poland, more or less at will.

SIGISMUND I (1467-1548), reigned 1506-1548. The son of KASIMIR, he ruled alone until 1530, when he was joined by his ten-year-old son and became referred to as 'The Old'.

SIGISMUND II (1520-1572), reigned 1530-1572. The last male Jagiellon, he co-ruled with his father, SIGISMUND I, for eighteen years. The last twenty years of his reign are sometimes called Poland's *Golden Age*. A year's interregnum followed his death.

HENRY (1551-1575), reigned 1573-1575. He was also HENRY III of France.

STEPHEN BATORY, of Transylvania (1522-1586), reigned 1575-1586. He was the son-in-law of SIGISMUND II. A year's interregnum followed.

SIGISMUND III, Vasa (1566-1632), reigned 1587-1632. the grandson of SIGISMUND I, he was SIGISMUND of Sweden for some of his ruling years.

VLADISLAV IV (1595-1648), son of SIGISMUND, reigned 1632-1648. He defended Poland brilliantly against attack from his father's erstwhile Swedish subjects, as well as keeping Russia and Turkey at bay.

JOHN II, Kasimir (1609-1668), reigned 1648-1668. The brother of

VLADISLAV, he was a Cardinal and lived in France until summoned to the throne when nearly forty. Poland was at a low ebb, hit by the plague, religious schism, crop failures and marauding neighbours. Eventually John could take no more and abdicated.

MICHAEL WISNIOWIECKI (1638-1673), reigned 1669-1673. It took a year to arrive at a unanimous vote electing him king. His father was a large landholder and acquired a good record for stemming waves of invading Cossacks.

JOHN III, Sobieski (1629-1696), reigned 1674-1696. With good French connections, both politically and through marriage, John became the greatest king Poland ever had. He was a general of genius. In 1683 he 'rescued' Vienna and destroyed the Turkish presence.

AUGUSTUS (1670-1733), reigned 1697-1704. Augustus was one of eighteen candidates for the throne when JOHN died. Technically he was Augustus II because SIGISMUND II was also referred to as Augustus I (see below).

STANISLAV I, Leszozynski (1677-1733), reigned 1704-1709. His pro-French attitude worried the Poles and he was deposed, but 'given' Lorraine, in France, as ample compensation. He returned to the Polish throne for eight months in 1733.

AUGUSTUS II, returned to the throne, 1709-1733, after STANISLAV had forced his abdication in 1704.

AUGUSTUS III (1796-1763), reigned 1733-1763. He was also Elector of Saxony and supported Prussia in the first Silesian War. He changed sides for the second Silesian conflict and had to pay Prussia an indemnity of one million rix-dollars.

STANISLAV II (1732-1798), reigned 1764-1795. He had once been one of CATHERINE of Russia's many lovers and succeeded to the throne of Poland through her influence. He was double-crossed by Catherine and Russia invaded Poland twice. Prussia, too, took action and by 1795, the country was virtually torn apart. In the November of that year, Stanislav abdicated. He died, virtually a prisoner, in Russia.

PORTUGAL

Though colonized by the Romans, Portugal did not become established as a kingdom until the end of the eleventh century. It was then under French domination, through the Burgundian House of Capet. Gradually it pushed southwards, driving the Moors out of the country as it expanded. The sixteenth century saw massive overseas growth and Portugal became an international power, with staggeringly rich colonies in India and Brazil. In 1580, all this wealth fell into the laps of the Spanish Habsburgs, who retained power until the emergence of the Braganzas in 1640. The Braganzas held the throne until the abolition of the monarchy in 1910. A republic was declared in August 1911.

Capital *LISBON*; currency *escudo*

ALFONSO I (1094-1185), reigned 1112-1185. His father, Count Henry of Burgundy, married the illegitimate daughter of ALFONSO of Leon. This strong-minded young woman brought her husband Portugal as her dowry. The seven-foot-tall (2.13 metres) Alfonso was styled as 'king' in 1139, having pushed the Moors back south of the river Tagus and Lisbon.

SANCHO I (1154-1211), reigned 1185-1211. In 1184 Sancho had to be rescued by his ninety-year-old father, ALFONSO, having landed in trouble besieging the Moors at Santarem.

ALFONSO II (1185-1223), son of SANCHO, reigned 1211-1223. In his avarice, he attempted to appropriate church revenues, which led him to be excommunicated by Pope Honorius III. Alfonso, 'The Fat', was as rotund as his grandfather was tall.

SANCHO II (1209-1248), reigned 1223-1248. As civil war boiled, Sancho had so little authority that the Pope let his brother, ALFONSO, depose him. When the unrest died down, Sancho went into exile for the last two years of his life, leaving Alfonso Regent.

ALFONSO III (1210-1279), reigned 1248-1279. He carried on ALFONSO II's campaign of Moor expulsion and added the Algarve region to the kingdom.

DIONSIUS, *Diniz* (1261-1325), reigned 1279-1325. The son of ALFONSO III, he founded the University of Coimbra.

ALFONSO IV (1291-1357), reigned 1325-1357. A spiteful man, he 'hastened' the death of his father, DIONSIUS, and organized the barbarous murder of his daughter-in-law, Inez.

PEDRO I (1320-1367), reigned 1357-1367. He revenged his wife's murder by devastating large tracts of the country between the Douro and Minho rivers, before being reconciled with his sadistic sire.

FERDINAND I, 'The Gentleman', *El Gentil* (born 1345), reigned 1367-1383. As a great-great-grandson of SANCHO II, he became a claimant to the throne of Castile and became involved in wars which lasted for twelve years, from 1370. The, eventual, *Peace of Badajoz* stipulated that his daughter, BEATRICE, should marry JOHN of Castile. Ferdinand was the last of the Portuguese Burgundian kings.

BEATRICE (dates unknown), reigned 1383-1385. The daughter of FERDINAND, she was the *de jure* Queen of Portugal. Her 'reign' ended when her faction was roundly defeated at Aljubarrota by JOHN's forces. Beatrice 'faded away' and no more is known of her.

JOHN, of Aviz (1357-1433), reigned 1385-1433. He was the illegitimate son of PEDRO and the father of Henry, 'The Navigator'. John established a relationship with England, which lasted so long that, in the twentieth century, Portugal is often referred to as 'Britain's oldest ally'.

EDWARD (1391-1438), son of JOHN, reigned 1433-1438.

ALFONSO V (1432-1481), reigned 1438-1481. He was called 'The African', as he extended his fight against the Moors into Africa itself – with mixed success. In 1475 he invaded Castile. He completely over-reached himself and abdicated in favour of his son, JOHN, who refused the crown, leaving his father to carry on for another two years. In 1478 it all became too much for him and he retired to a monastery at Cintra.

JOHN II (1455-1495), reigned 1481-1495. 'The Perfect Prince' seemed perfectly lacking in scruples. He was the ruthless son of ALFONSO. During his reign his subject, Diaz, discovered the Cape of Good Hope and Portuguese colonization began on the Gold Coast of Africa.

MANUEL I (1469-1521), reigned 1495-1521. The nephew of ALFONSO V, he claimed Brazil for Portugal, created rich trade, through Goa, with India and established a Congolese kingdom.

JOHN III (1502-1557), son of MANUEL, reigned 1521-1557. He was dominated by the Church and the commercial effect on his country was disastrous.

SEBASTIAN (1554-1578), JOHN's grandson, reigned 1557-1578. He was killed while 'crusading' in Morocco. His slightly mysterious life started a sort of 'Fake Sebastian' industry. Men masquerading as Sebastian appeared regularly for years after 1578. One such, '...a queer youth of humble birth', the son of a potter, who travelled around Portugal in 1584 peddling rosaries, told innkeepers that he was King Sebastian and 'obtained gratuitous hospitality'.

HENRY (1512-1580), reigned 1578-1580. He was the last of the Aziz dynasty. He effectively ended the line upon being made a cardinal in 1542. He may have been a pillar of the Church, but he was a broken reed of state. A Council of Regency was appointed and ruled after his death for five months.

PHILIP I (1527-1598), reigned 1580-1598. JOHN III's son-in-law, he was PHILIP II of Spain and husband of Queen MARY of England.

PHILIP II (1578-1621), reigned 1598-1621. He was PHILIP III of Spain.

PHILIP III (1605-1640), reigned 1621-1640. The son of PHILIP II (or III of Spain) he was PHILIP IV of Spain and the last Portuguese Habsburg.

JOHN IV, 'The Fortunate' (1604-1656), reigned 1640-1656. The first of the Braganzas, he was the great-great-grandson of MANUEL I.

ALFONSO VI (1643-1683), reigned 1656-1683. The son of JOHN, he suffered from a particularly nasty form of insanity. For the last 27 years of his life his wife and brother had him committed to confinement on the island of Terceira. There he became so fat, he had to be rolled along the passages of his house.

PEDRO II (1648-1706), reigned 1683-1706. He was the brother of the regrettable ALFONSO and had married Alfonso's wife after arranging a trumped-up, nullity divorce.

JOHN V (1689-1750), reigned 1706-1750. Despite the truly immense flow of silver coming in from Brazil, PEDRO's son managed to spend it all, and more, on the Portuguese contemporary equivalent of wine, women and song.

JOSEPH (1714–1777), reigned 1750–1777. The son of the fleshly JOHN, Joseph was a withdrawn, indolent man. He was more than happy to leave matters of state to his statesman, Pombal, who, in 1750, aged 51, was at the height of his power.

MARIA I (1734–1816), reigned 1777–1816. JOSEPH's daughter, most of the time she was mentally unbalanced. Her husband, PEDRO III, the son of her uncle JOHN, ruled with her until 1786, when he died aged 69. In 1807, she was removed to Brazil and Portugal was administered by the Duke of Wellington and his diplomatic staff.

JOHN VI, Prince of Brazil (1767–1826), reigned 1816–1826. The son of MARIA and PEDRO II, he had been his demented mother's regent since 1799. He ruled Portugal from Brazil until 1822, then stayed in Lisbon for the last four years of his reign. He granted Brazil independence in 1825.

PEDRO IV (1798–1834), reigned in 1826. The elder son of JOHN VI, he was King of Portugal for only sixty days. He became PEDRO I, Emperor of Brazil.

MARIA II (1819–1853), reigned 1826–1853. She was the eldest daughter of PEDRO IV, but was deposed by her uncle MIGUEL, after less than two years on the throne. She returned after MIGUEL's death in 1834 and reigned, as the last Braganza, until 1853.

MIGUEL (1802–1866), reigned 1828–1834. The younger son of JOHN VI, a dashing man, deposed his niece MARIA II (for whom he was Regent). He was deposed himself in 1834 and died in Germany, thirty-two years later.

PEDRO V (1837–1861), reigned 1853–1861. The eldest son of MARIA and her husband FERDINAND (of Saxe-Coburg).

LUIS (1838–1889), PEDRO V's brother, reigned 1861–1889. During his longish reign, the growth of republicanism became more evident than ever before.

CHARLES (1863–1908), reigned 1889–1908. Despite the growing radical element and Charles's 'flamboyant' behaviour, LUIS's elder son was popular. It could not last, however, and in February 1908 he and his son and heir, Luis, were assassinated as they drove through Lisbon in an open carriage.

MANUEL II (1889–1932), reigned 1908–1910. The younger son of CHARLES, Manuel fled to Gibraltar, and from thence to England, when revolution broke out after the general election of 1910. He died in Twickenham.

POWYS

From the sixth century, Powys was a principality in north central Wales. Some 300 years later it was united with Gwynedd, gaining a form of independence in 1075. It split into north and south in 1160 and was ruled by the grandsons of Bleddyn, until the death of Gruffydd Maelor in 1269.

BLEDDYN AP CYNFYN (c.1025-1075), reigned 1063-1075. He was the half-brother of Prince Gruffyd ap Rhys, who, as a prince, was Ruler of All Wales. (Gruffyd was murdered in 1063 and his head sent to the Anglo Saxon Earl, HAROLD, as a present.) Bleddyn ruled together with his brother Rhiwallon, who was killed in 1073. He ruled alone for a further two years before he, too, was cut down and the kingdom passed to his son, Madog ap Bleddyn, who reigned as a prince, not king.

PRUSSIA

Geographically, what was once the Baltic coastal region of Prussia now lies largely in Poland. Once it was the most powerful element in the German Empire. At the Reformation, the last Grand Master of the Teutonic Knights became a Lutheran and created himself Duke of Prussia in the east. In 1618, the territory of Brandenburg was added and the Hohenzollerns became leaders of a whole kingdom in 1701.

Capital *BERLIN*

FREDERICK I (1657-1713), reigned 1701-1713. The son of the Elector of Brandenburg, Frederick William, whom he succeeded as Frederick III in 1688, he was crowned first King of Prussia in 1701. He founded the University at Halle and the Academy of Sciences, yet he lived grandiosely. He supported a vastly oversized standing army and further bankrupted his treasury by having to maintain splendid palaces.

FREDERICK-WILLIAM I (1688-1740), reigned 1713-1740. As careful over expenditure as his father, FREDERICK I, had been lavish, he expanded his kingdom by acquiring Stettin and part of Pomerania, under the *Peace of Stockholm* in 1720. It was Frederick-William who laid the foundation for the military might of Prussia which followed.

FREDERICK II, 'The Great' (1712-1786), reigned 1740-1786. This military genius (who looked anything but a soldier) was the grandson of GEORGE I of England. He raised his country into a great and respected European power. He was also a friend of Voltaire and published a number of books. By the last decade of his reign, gout and '...infirmities almost inseparably attendant on his period of life, ...indeed enfeebled his legs'.

FREDERICK-WILLIAM II (1744-1797), reigned 1786-1797. The nephew of FREDERICK, 'The Great', in an otherwise unmemorable reign, he formed an alliance with Austria in 1792.

FREDERICK-WILLIAM III (1770-1840), reigned 1797-1840. Luckily, this nervy son of FREDERICK-WILLIAM II had three strong councillors in Scharnhorst, Stein and Hardenburg to help him cope with the aggressive NAPOLEON, against whom war was declared in 1806. Princess Catherine Radziwill wrote that Frederick-William '...could never have been a handsome man but in age he was imposing'.

FREDERICK-WILLIAM IV (1795-1861), reigned 1840-1861. He succeeded his father, but was not as highly strung as he. He was compelled to grant a constitution in 1848. Not long after, he became so physically incapacitated, he was obliged to hand over to his brother, William, who became Regent in 1858.

WILLIAM I (born 1797), reigned 1861-1871. Ten years after he came to the throne, the German Empire was established.

ROMANIA

Spelt Romania by its present masters, it was previously spelt Roumania or Rumania. An ethnic curiosity, Romanians can probably claim Roman ancestry. The people who made up a Wallachian state in this territory, in the late 1200s, were a migrant, mix-blooded lot. They were joined to Moldavia, the second state, established about a hundred years later. The governors of these little principalities were called *Voivodes*. The country suffered the fate of most Balkan states, when the Turks took over in the 16th century. They were eventually forced to grant the country autonomy. A Hohenzollern prince was elected Prince of Roumania, and recognized by the *Treaty of Berlin* in July 1878. After 1918, Romania was greatly enlarged when Transylvania was added to it. Russia retrieved the latter in 1940 and by 1947 the communist takeover was completed. The country became the Romanian People's Republic.

Capital *BUCHAREST*; currency *leu*

CAROL I (1839-1914), reigned 1881-1914. He was Prince Charles of Hohenzollern-Sigmaringen, first Prince of Roumania in 1886 and King in 1881.

FERDINAND I (1865-1927), reigned 1914-1927. The nephew of CAROL, he was at the head of his armies in the *Bulgarian Campaign* of 1913. It was during his reign that universal suffrage was introduced.

MICHAEL (born 1921), reigned 1927-1930. His father, CAROL II, renounced the throne, so the six-year-old Michael was placed upon it and a Regent appointed.

CAROL II (1893-1953), reigned 1930-1940. The eldest son of FERDINAND (and a great-grandson of Queen VICTORIA) Carol was a wilful, dissolute man. He made a morganatic marriage to Jeanne Lambrino, a general's daughter, before marrying Helen of Greece, by whom he had MICHAEL, in 1921. In 1925 he eloped with his mistress, Magda Lupescu, and renounced the throne. But in 1920, exhibiting typical impetuosity, he came back to Bucharest and deposed Michael. The pressures were too great. In 1940 he abdicated and seven years later married Lupescu in Brazil. He died in Lisbon; she lasted another 24 years.

MICHAEL returned to the throne, 1940-1947. After 1945, having played a part in overthrowing Antonescu, who had been head of state during the Nazi occupation, Michael, by then 25, found the communist regime intolerable. Before he could be deposed, he abdicated. He was granted Romanian citizenship and US$100,000. He married Anne of Bourbon-Parma in 1948 and they had five daughters. His money did not last long and at one stage, he was a salesman for the Lockheed Aircraft Company.

RUSSIA

The USSR of today is very much larger than even the vast territory which formed the kingdom of the last Tsar in 1917, the year he was deposed. During the ninth century, the state of Kiev grew powerful, having been a focal colonizing area for the Slavic tribes which moved across the land adjoining the Caspian, Black and Baltic seas. Gradually the emphasis moved north to Moscow, which was the eventual nucleus of Russia. A state based on Moscow was clearly in evidence by the reign of Alexander Nevsky (1238-1252) the first ruler of the Rurik dynasty. IVAN, 'The Terrible', was from the same house, at the time the Russian Princes became Russian Tsars, in 1547.

Capital (today) *MOSCOW*; currency *rouble*

IVAN IV, 'The Terrible' (1530-1584), reigned 1533-1584. The only son of Basil III, he became Tsar in 1547. Orphaned at seven, Ivan was brought up in a brutal atmosphere and grew to live a brutal life. Despite fearful rages (during one of which he killed his beloved son, Ivan, in 1580) savage sexual lust and a psychopathic nature, he would listen to the case for the 'underdog' with patience. He had (definitely) seven wives, but only two sons survived. While his fifth wife was still alive he was negotiating his marriage to Mary Hastings, one of the ladies of the court of Queen ELIZABETH of England. Despite his mental imbalance, he had political foresight (almost anticipating the idealistic PETER, 'The Great') and was, at heart, a cultured and hard-working man.

FEODOR (1557-1598), reigned 1584-1598. The son of IVAN, he was the last of the House of Rurik. During his reign the Russian Church was split from Constantinople and a Russian Patriarchate established. To put it mildly, Feodor was very feeble-minded.

IRINA (1560-1603), reigned in 1598. FEODOR's widow, she reigned in name only from January 7-17, 1598. She became a nun. She is significant in that BORIS GODUNOV was her brother.

BORIS GODUNOV (1552-1605), reigned 1598-1605. He was the first of the House of Godunov. The chief member of the Regency, which had been a necessity during the reign of the idiotic FEODOR, although he was elected to rule, he was never really regarded as anything but an upstart. There was a strong possibility that Boris had a hand in disposing of the *Czarevitch* Dmitri, Feodor's son and heir.

FEODOR II (1589-1605), reigned in 1605. The son of BORIS, he was brutally murdered by a Moscow mob, only two months after succeeding his father.

DIMITRI (1581-1606), reigned 1605-1606. He was usually called 'The False Dimitri'. He claimed to be the son of IVAN, 'The Terrible'. Impostor or not, he led the revolt against BORIS and, in the eleven months of his reign, at least *suggested* a number of humanitarian reforms.

VASILI IV, Shuisky (1552-1612), reigned 1606-1610. The one and only Shuisky Tsar, he led the revolt which unseated DIMITRI. He fared no better. In 1610 he, too, was deposed and he died in a monastery two years later. He was the son of Prince Dimitri III of Nizhny Novgorod.

MICHAEL (1596-1645), reigned 1613-1645. He was the first of the Romanovs. IVAN, 'The Terrible's' first wife was a Zakharina-Koshkina, a surname later known as Romanov. Michael was a great nephew of the Tsarina Anastasia.

ALEXEI (1629-1676), reigned 1645-1676. His warlike reign showed a net gain of Eastern Siberia. He codified the laws of many Russian provinces and gradually began to introduce 'civilizing touches' from western Europe.

FEODOR III (1661-1682), reigned 1676-1682. He was the son of ALEXEI. An undistinguished man, he did not live long enough to keep his disastrous younger brother off the throne.

IVAN V (1666-1696), reigned 1682-1696. FEODOR's half-brother was a half blind, half-witted, drooling degenerate. He was used as a tool to keep his brother PETER off the throne and allow the power to be in the hands of Ivan's half-sister, Sophia. Despite his handicaps, Ivan married and fathered five daughters.

PETER I, 'The Great' (1672-1725), reigned 1682-1725. Technically he was the last Tsar, as he became Emperor in 1721. From the very beginning of his full-brother, IVAN's reign, it was obvious that the older boy was totally incapable and Peter was accepted as co-ruler, though he was never officially a regent. He was, by any standards, a remarkable man. When he was 26, he went to London to study (and roister). He was described, on that visit, as being tall but had '...convulsions, sometimes of the eyes, sometimes in his arms and sometimes in his whole body...Then he has spasms in his legs so that he can hardly stand still in one place'. He, like so many things Russian, was a complex of contrasts. He introduced much 'Western culture' – yet had his own son, a pale, poor fellow of 28, beaten to death in prison; he founded the superb city of St Petersburg – yet ruled by terror. He defeated Sweden at Poltava in 1709 and under him the giant that was Russia began to come awake.

CATHERINE (1679-1727), reigned 1725-1727. The widow of PETER, née Skowronska, she rose from Lithuanian laundrywoman to Tsar's consort, before becoming Empress. The style of Emperor was adopted in 1721 and PETER was, in name, the last Tsar. A bawdy, young woman, she became PETER's mistress in 1703 and was married to him four years later. She later founded the Russian Academy of Sciences.

PETER II (1715-1730), reigned 1727-1730. He was the son of 'The Great's' murdered son, Alexis.

ANNE (1693-1740), reigned 1730-1740. The youngest surviving daughter of IVAN V and sister of PETER I, she was elected by the Secret High Council on the understanding that they called the tune. She double-crossed them and it was a German ('of low birth') called Biren who really called the tune. The Secret High Council members – eight of the chief nobles of Russia – all 'disappeared'.

IVAN VI (1740-1764), reigned 1740-1741. ANNE adopted the eight-week-old boy, her great-nephew, just twelve days before she died, and named him her heir. ANNE's lover, Biren, was ousted from a Regency in less than a month. Ivan's own mother, Leopoldovna of Mecklenburg, handed the authority to vice-Chancellor Osterman. The whole family were imprisoned and a *coup d'état* put ELIZABETH on the throne. Poor Ivan was kept chained in solitary confinement for twenty years, lost his reason (not unnaturally) and was eventually murdered on CATHERINE, 'The Great's', orders.

ELIZABETH (1709-1762), reigned 1741-1762. She was PETER, 'The Great's', only surviving daughter. Fleshy and fashionable, Elizabeth founded the University of Moscow. In 1760, her armies pressed FREDERICK, 'The Great', of Prussia right back into Berlin.

PETER III (1728-1762), reigned in 1762. Grandson of PETER, 'The Great', and born at Kiel, he ought more properly to be called Karl Peter Ulrich. He married CATHERINE in 1745, made peace with FREDERICK, 'The Great', and was murdered for his pains after only a few months on the throne. This left a clear field for the not over-scrupulous Catherine.

CATHERINE II (1729-1796), reigned 1762-1796. The object of her marriage to PETER was to produce an heir for Russia. Since PETER was mad, impotent and/or sterile, Catherine was not, at first, successful. She did produce a son in 1755, but the father was probably Sergei Saltykov, one of the first of her procession of lovers. Catherine was probably the worst thing to happen to Russia since the Flood, although Voltaire, commenting on her influence, said that 'light now comes from the north'. She disposed of the country of Poland almost as effectively as she disposed of her lovers (which she continued to take until she was well over 60).

PAUL (1754-1801), reigned 1796-1801. He was CATHERINE's son (by PETER?). His legitimacy had only a short period in which it could be put to the test, since he was assassinated less than five years after succeeding.

ALEXANDER I (1777-1825), reigned 1801-1825. He was PAUL's son. He abolished serfdom in the Baltic provinces and introduced many ameliorating reforms. It was his Russia that put an end to NAPOLEON's expansion eastwards. As a result he has sometimes been referred to as the 'Liberator of Europe'.

NICHOLAS I (1796-1855), reigned 1825-1855. PAUL's third son was concerned with improving Russia by introducing a good railway system, improving hospitals, and liberating serfs. Privately, he was a devoted family man. Compared to his predecessors, Nicholas would appear to be a positive paragon. He was, however, very autocratic and surprisingly intolerant. He lived long enough to see his country fighting England in the senseless *Crimean War*.

ALEXANDER II (1845-1881), reigned 1855-1881. At the second attempt, the Anarchists managed to murder him. This was really a self-inflicted misfortune, as this plump and friendly man was about to grant a very liberal (by Russian standards) new constitution to his people.

ALEXANDER III (1845-1894), reigned 1881-1894. Despite the swelling tide of revolution and Alexander's hardly benevolent attitude to his subjects, his reign saw general material prosperity in the country and less evidence of terrorist and anarchistic activity, than in his father's foreshortened reign.

NICHOLAS (1868-1918), reigned 1894-1918. ALEXANDER's eldest, amiable and inept son bore a most striking physical resemblance to GEORGE V of Great Britain. (George's mother, Alexandra, was a princess of Denmark. Her sister, Dagmar, married Nicholas's father, making George and Nicholas first cousins.) Whatever had held the revolution in check during his father's reign broke loose in the first years of the twentieth century. Nicholas was dominated by his wife, Alexandra Feodorovna, and she was completely absorbed in the health of their only son, the haemophiliac heir to the throne. (The haemophilia came through Queen VICTORIA: the Tsarina was Alix of Hesse, Victoria's granddaughter.) The family fell into the hands of the licentious monk, Rasputin, who seemed to be able to alleviate the little boy's sufferings somewhat. A disastrous war with Japan, in 1904, fed the flames and in 1917, the Tsar and his family were placed under house arrest at Tsarskoe Selo. In April 1918, they were all taken to Ekaterinburg in the Urals and there, probably on July 17, the entire family were shot, without trial, and their bodies burnt.

SARDINIA

In 1720, the Duchy of Savoy, to which the island had just been ceded, permitted a kingdom to be created under the Treaty of London. So Sardinia was joined to Nice, Savoy and Piedmont, Liguria being added after the Napoleonic Wars. In 1859 and 1860, Lombardy, the Two Sicilies, the Papal Legations and the Central Duchies were attached and the Kingdom of Italy came into being.

VICTOR AMADEUS II, of Savoy (1666-1732), reigned 1720-1730. He was the first King of Sardinia. His father, Duke Charles, died when he was nine and he was brought up by his bossy mother, Jeanne (*Madama Reale*) and began to govern Savoy himself, when he was sixteen. By the *Treaty of Utrecht* in 1713, the Kingdom of Sicily was given to Victor, but three years later, he was obliged, by the *Quadruple Alliance* to exchange Sicily for Sardinia. Widowed, he remarried, but his second wife caused trouble between him and his son CHARLES, who actually had his father arrested after his abdication. He died at Moncalieri, where his son had him imprisoned.

CHARLES-EMANUEL III (1701-1773), reigned 1730-1773. Victor's unfilial first-born spent his reign involved in almost continuous conflict. He led his armies against, amongst others, Austria. As a result, he was able to pass on a powerful, expanding and wealthy kingdom to his son.

VICTOR AMADEUS III (1726-1796), reigned 1773-1796. He lost Savoy and Nice in 1792 and, by the end of his reign, was obliged to make a disadvantageous peace with NAPOLEON.

CHARLES-EMANUEL IV (1751-1819), reigned 1796-1802. He succeeded his father, VICTOR, on a 'slippery throne' and, before six years were out, had abdicated it to his younger brother and become a monk.

VICTOR-EMANUEL I (1759-1824), reigned 1802-1821. In 1814 he returned to Turin and the *Congress of Vienna* granted him the Genoese territory. However, he was unable to deal with an aristocratic rebellion and, having no sons of his own, abdicated in favour of his younger brother.

CHARLES-FELIX (1765-1831), reigned 1821-1831. Supported by Austria, he restored the stability of his throne and set about making a number of improvements (including many new roads) in the kingdom. He died without male issue and the throne passed to a cousin of the Carignano branch of the family.

CHARLES ALBERT (1798-1849), reigned 1831-1849. He was a collateral relative of CHARLES-FELIX (actually a grandson, five times removed, of Charles Emanuel I of Savoy, who died in 1630). He failed to defeat the Austrians over Lombardy and abdicated, dying in Oporto four months later.

VICTOR-EMANUEL (born 1820), reigned 1849-1861. The son of CHARLES ALBERT, he became the first King of Italy in 1861.

SAXONY

The 'home of the Saxons', literally, this region of northern Germany was conquered by Charlemagne. Its eventual rulers (who were styled Dukes) obtained the Imperial crown in the tenth century. It became an electorate in 1423, was split between two branches of the Wettin family in 1485, reunited in 1547 and elevated to a kingdom in 1806.

Capital *DRESDEN*

FREDERICK AUGUSTUS I (1750-1827), reigned 1750-1827. He was the son of FREDERICK II, King of Poland and grandson of Augustus, Elector of Saxony ('...an indolent prince'). Frederick Augustus paid six million florins for the land which became his kingdom. He increased its area after the *Treaty of Posen* by an alliance with France. When he was 28, someone wrote of this King-to-be: 'Coldness and inanimation characterize his behaviour...he displays none of the gracious and communicative disposition which...characterize...his three contemporaries'.

ANTHONY CLEMENT (1755-1836), brother of FREDERICK, reigned 1827-1836.

FREDERICK AUGUSTUS II (1797-1854), reigned 1836-1854. He had been Regent to his uncle ANTHONY since 1830.

JOHN (1801-1873), reigned 1854-1873. FREDERICK's brother and a notable Dante scholar, he published his translation of the *Divina Commedia* in 1839.

ALBERT (1828-1902), reigned 1873-1902. The son of JOHN, he commanded an army corps in the Franco-German War while Crown Prince.

GEORGE (1832-1904), reigned 1902-1904. The younger brother of ALBERT, he married Dona Maria, the Infanta of Portugal.

FREDERICK AUGUSTUS III (born 1865), reigned 1904-1918. The last king of Saxony, he was dethroned in 1918 and given compensation of 300,000 marks.

 # SCOTLAND

Scotland became a kingdom in 843, when Kenneth, who had been King of Dalradia for two years, became King of the Picts and therefore of Scotland. Before him there had been Kings of *Alba* and the very first Scottish dynasty was called Alba rather than MacAlpin, his family name. The king was 'King of the Scots', rather than 'King of Scotland', which was only used briefly by Balliol between 1292 and 1306.

Capital *EDINBURGH*; currency *pound sterling* but some Scottish banks produce their own currency.

MALCOLM II (born 954), reigned 1005-1034. He was actually the sixteenth King of the Scots and still of MacAlpin descent, being a son of Kenneth II, who died in 995. In his reign, Scotland achieved approximately the same territorial size as its area today.

DUNCAN I (died 1040), reigned 1034-1040. MALCOLM's brother, he was murdered by MACBETH, his cousin.

MACBETH (died 1057), reigned 1040-1057. He was eventually killed by DUNCAN's son near Aberdeen. He had been defeated by Siward at Dunsinane and was the model for Shakespeare's *Macbeth*. Although his real wife, Gruoch, granddaughter of Kenneth II, was almost certainly neither a sleepwalker nor a murderess.

LULACH (died 1058), reigned 1057-1058. Called 'The Simple', he was MACBETH's stepson and was also disposed of by MALCOLM.

MALCOLM III (1031-1093), Duncan's son, reigned 1058-1093. Having made his way to the throne by disposing of his two predecessors, he spent most of his long reign fighting border wars. He was known as *Canmore* which meant 'Great Chief'. His wife, Margaret, the daughter of EDMUND of England, influenced Malcolm considerably and her virtue led her to be canonized as a Saint in 1250. He invaded England and was killed in battle at Alnwick.

DONALD III, called *Donald Bane* (1033–1099), reigned 1093–1094. He was MALCOLM III's younger brother and sneakily deposed by his nephew DUNCAN II. He died five years later, having been blinded by another nephew, EDGAR.

DUNCAN II (1060–1094), reigned in 1094. He was murdered at the behest of his half-brother, EDMUND (their father, MALCOLM, had been twice married).

EDMUND (dates unknown), reigned 1094–1097. He ruled jointly with a restored DONALD until they were both deposed by EDGAR, MALCOLM III's seventh son. He became a monk and died some years later.

EDGAR (1074–1107), reigned 1097–1107. He only managed to secure the throne with the strong support of the English, whose vassal he became.

ALEXANDER (1077–1124), reigned 1107–1124. He was yet another of MALCOLM's sons. He was a vassal of HENRY I of England and married, Sybilla, Henry's illegitimate daughter.

DAVID I (1080–1153), reigned 1124–1153. The ninth and youngest son of MALCOLM he became St David. His feast day is on March 24. Very anglicized, David founded Abbeys, gave vast tracts of land to the Church (which was why he was canonized) and introduced a sound 'money economy' to Scotland.

MALCOLM IV (1142–1165), reigned 1153–1165. The grandson of St DAVID, he was obliged to hand Northumbria and Cumbria back to England after his surrender to HENRY II at Chester in 1157. He was so effeminate, he was called 'The Maiden' behind his back. (Despite this he fathered one illegitimate son.)

WILLIAM I, 'The Lion' (1145–1214), reigned 1165–1214. He invaded England, but was no more successful than brother MALCOLM. He was captured, forced to pay homage to HENRY II and released in 1175.

ALEXANDER II (1198–1249), reigned 1214–1249. 'The Lion's' son, he married King JOHN's daughter and renounced all Scottish claims to Cumbria and Northumbria.

ALEXANDER III (1241–1286), reigned 1249–1286. The last MacAlpin, he was ALEXANDER's son by his second marriage. He secured the Western Isles from Norway, but on March 19, 1286, while looking out to sea at Kinghorn in Fife, he dismounted from his horse rather carelessly and fell over a cliff to his death.

MARGARET, 'The Maid of Norway' (1283–1290), reigned 1286–1290. She was ALEXANDER's granddaughter, by his only daughter and ERIK II of Norway. She is almost certainly the only monarch in the world to have died from seasickness. In September 1290, she set sail from Norway to take over her new kingdom, but the convoy had to put into the Orkneys, as the child Queen was too ill to sail on, and there she died.

From September 1290–1292, came the first of two interregnums. King EDWARD I of England, 'The Hammer of the Scots', asked for claimants to the throne and thirteen men stepped forward. Eventually Edward chose JOHN BALLIOL, as he hoped that he would be a puppet king for him in this troublesome region.

JOHN BALLIOL, or Baliol (1250–1313), reigned 1292–1296. He was the great-great-great-grandson of DAVID I. His father and mother, Devorguilla, founded Balliol College, Oxford, in about 1265. In 1296 he was obliged to surrender the throne and went to live in Normandy. From July 1296 to March 1306, there was a second interregnum. The Scots, under William Wallace (who was executed in London in 1305) led the nationalists against the English efforts to subdue the country. The struggle was continued by ROBERT after Wallace's death.

ROBERT I, 'The Bruce' (1274–1329), reigned 1306–1329. He was the first of the Bruce dynasty. After early setbacks, Robert completely routed the English army at the *Battle of Bannockburn* in June 1314. In 1328, England renounced all claims to Scotland and Robert rebuilt his nation. As active off the throne, as on it, he sired at least five bastards, but had only one legal son who survived. He died mysteriously, probably of leprousy. His heart was cut out and taken to the Holy Land, but later brought back and buried in Melrose Abbey. (The rest of him lies in Dunfermline.)

DAVID II (1324–1371), reigned 1329–1371. Compared to his father, ROBERT, David grew to be a mean man, lacking courage. He was deposed by EDWARD BALLIOL in 1332 and six years of civil war followed. David first fled to France, then invaded England in 1346. He was captured and imprisoned for eleven years, before being ransomed. (At his otherwise unceremonious coronation, he was anointed with Holy Oil; the first time such a ritual had been enacted in Scotland. The oil was sent by Pope John XXII, who charged 12,000 florins for it.) David's first wife was daughter of JOHN of England.

EDWARD BALLIOL (died 1363), reigned 1332–1338. He was the son of JOHN BALLIOL. With English support, Edward was able to depose DAVID. Civil war continued in Scotland and Edward fled in 1338. DAVID returned in 1340 and ruled (more or less) until his death.

ROBERT II (1316–1390), reigned 1371–1390. A grandson of ROBERT, 'The Bruce' (and a half-brother of DAVID II) he was the first of the Steward dynasty. He was nicknamed 'The Steward' and later 'King Bleare', because of his bloodshot eyes. A weak man, his kingdom collapsed around him.

ROBERT III (1337–1406), reigned 1390–1406. He was born about ten years before his father, ROBERT II, married his mother, and was christened·John. Already a bit weak in the head, a kick from a horse loosened the rest up there and Scotland sank lower than it ever had during the reign of his incompetent father. He was popularly supposed to have died of shock on being told that his son James, who was sent to France for safety, had been captured by the English en route.

JAMES I (1396-1437), reigned 1406-1437. Unwittingly the cause of his father's death (though the rumour was probably started by the Scots as anti-English propaganda) James was ransomed in 1423. A good ruler and a man of the arts, in a few years he achieved much. He was murdered by his uncle, the Earl of Atholl.

JAMES II (1430-1460), reigned 1437-1460. Having regained much ground lost by his father, JAMES I, James was accidentally killed by a prematurely exploding cannon, whilst his army was trying to repossess the town of Roxburgh from the English. His nickname was 'Fiery Face'.

JAMES III (1452-1488), reigned 1460-1488. Bad luck, a disastrous famine and bad management attended the reign. He was killed whilst fleeing the field, having been defeated by rebellious Scottish lords at Sauchieburn.

JAMES IV (1473-1513), reigned 1488-1513. The son of JAMES III, he was killed with the 'Flowers of the Forest' (in other words most of the better elements of the Scottish hierarchy) at the bloody *Battle of Flodden Field* on September 9. He had married Margaret, daughter of HENRY VII of England, a significant alliance.

JAMES V (1512-1542), reigned 1513-1542. The only surviving son of JAMES V, he could not control his nobles. He married Madeline, daughter of FRANCIS I of France.

MARY, 'Queen of Scots' (1542-1567), reigned 1542-1567. The oversexed, unscrupulous and only daughter of JAMES V, she married the Dauphin of France. He became King FRANCIS in 1559 and died seventeen months later, leaving Mary an eighteen-year-old widow. Now the Dowager Queen of Catholic France, she returned to Scotland and, in 1565, married the thin-legged Lord Darnley, by whom she had a son. On February 10, 1567, she contrived her stupid husband's murder, by having blown him up in his bed. She then married Earl Bothwell, the man who had murdered him. Her way of life alienated her from her people. She went south to England, where she was equally unwelcome and a threat to the security of the English throne of Queen ELIZABETH. She was imprisoned and, after numerous escapades, which have been shamefully romanticized over the intervening 400 years, was eventually beheaded in Fotheringay Castle.

JAMES VI (1566-1625), reigned 1567-1625. The son of Mary, he was the last king of a separate Scotland. He became JAMES I of England in 1603, when ELIZABETH, the last Tudor, died (see Great Britain).

SERBIA

A region of Yugoslavia, it was established as a kingdom before 1200 by the Nemanjich family, who had thrown off the oppressive Byzantines. They stayed in power until 1389, when the Ottoman Turks poured in and instituted a regime. This lasted, more or less, until 1804, when Czerny George drove them out. They returned eight years later and Milosh Obrenovitch (who became the Prince in 1817) drove them out again in 1815 and Serbia became practically independent. After the First World War, Serbia merged with other Slavic peoples to form Yugoslavia.

Capital *BELGRADE*

STEPHEN NEMANYA (died 1196), reigned 1168-1196. He became the *Grand Zhupan* of Rashka and united the various states, except Bosnia, under his rule, though he never styled himself as king. He abdicated and became monk Simeon in the monastery on Mount Athos.

STEPHEN NEMANYA II (died 1227), reigned 1196-1227. He was also Grand Zhupan and then declared King in 1217.

STEPHEN RADOSLAV III (died 1234), reigned 1227-1234.

STEPHEN VLADISLAV IV (died 1243), reigned 1234-1243.

STEPHEN UROSH I (died 1277), reigned 1243-1276. He was christened Dragoslav. He gave up his throne and retired to a monastery for the last year of his life.

STEPHEN DRAGUTIN VI (1243-1317), reigned 1276-1282. He was deposed and, in exile, chose to become the Duke of Mačra.

STEPHEN UROSH MILUTIN II (died 1321), reigned 1282-1321. He was the son of STEPHEN UROSH I and Helen of Constantinople.

STEPHEN UROSH III (died 1331), the son of MILUTIN, reigned 1321-1331.

STEPHEN UROSH DUSHAN IV (1308-1355), reigned 1331-1355. (*Dushan* is a term of endearment derived from *dusha* the soul.) Stephen was illegitimate. A great soldier, in 1345 he proclaimed himself Emperor by conquest.

STEPHEN UROSH V (died 1371), reigned 1355-1371. DUSHAN's only son, he was the last of the Nemanjichs. The country drifted under Turkish rule and remained a *pashalik* of that oppressive empire, for nearly 350 years.

MILAN I (1854-1901), reigned 1882-1889. The third of the Obrenoviches, Milan was amoral, neurasthenic and two-faced. His public quarrels with Queen Natalie weakened a frail position and he was forced to abdicate.

ALEXANDER I (1876-1903), reigned 1889-1903. As he was only 13 when his father MILAN abdicated, his reign began under a regency of three generals. Alexander ejected this military trio when he was 17. He was a short, sulky, myopic man, who married his mistress, an engineer's widow. His people had no use for their king, so murdered him, his Queen Draga *and* her brother, for good measure. A cabinet of regicides was then formed to try and run the country.

PETER I (1844-1921), reigned 1903-1918. The eldest son of Alexander Karageorgevitch he had been elected Prince of Serbia in 1842. In 1918 he was elected PETER I of Yugoslavia.

SICILY

In very ancient times the island was controlled both from Carthage and Greece, but early in the ninth century AD, the Muslims took over from the Byzantines. This power broke up more or less naturally and the Hautevilles moved in. By 1130, King Roger was controlling Southern Italy, as well as Sicily. In 1194, the Hohenstauffens gained dominance. Then the kingdom fell to the French Angevins, but a rebellion in 1282 installed the Aragonese. They also acquired the Kingdom of Naples and both kingdoms passed to the Habsburgs, until their Spanish branch dwindled, when they passed to the Spanish Bourbons. The kingdom was finally absorbed by Italy.

Capital *PALERMO*

ROGER II (1095-1154), reigned 1130-1154. Having been Count of Sicily for 25 years, Roger was the first leader to be styled as 'King'. By skill and diplomatic *finesse* he built up the Kingdom of the Two Sicilies, incorporating Naples, and created an enviable bureaucratic service, staffed with Arabic personnel.

WILLIAM I, 'The Bad' (1120-1166), despite being ROGER's son, he was badly served by his favourite minister, Admiral Majone.

WILLIAM II, 'The Good' (1154-1189), reigned 1166-1189. 'The Good', like his father, 'The Bad', supported Pope Alexander III in his running fight with FREDERICK 'Barbarossa' – the Holy Roman Emperor.

TANCRED (died 1194), reigned 1189-1194. The illegitimate son of ROGER II's son, Roger, and styled the Count of Lecce.

WILLIAM III (1184-1194), reigned in 1194. TANCRED's son, he only ruled for ten months, under the regency of his mother, Queen Sibylla, and was probably murdered. He was the last of the Hauteville dynasty.

HENRY VI (1165-1197), reigned 1194-1197. King of Germany and

Emperor of the Holy Roman Empire, he ruled jointly with Queen Constanza, 'The Cruel'.

FREDERICK I (1194-1250), reigned 1197-1250. He became FREDERICK II of Germany in 1215. Frederick took over from his mother Constanza. In 1208, he began to rule 'in the Norman manner', but under the guardianship of Pope Innocent III. At the age of 13, Frederick was observed to have been given by 'the Universal Author of Nature...robust limbs and a strong body with which his vigorous spirit can achieve whatever he undertakes...'.

CONRAD I (1228-1254), reigned 1250-1254. He was also CONRAD IV of Germany and King of Jerusalem. (Upon Conrad's death there was much Papal manoeuvring. Eventually Pope Urban managed to place MANFRED on the throne, despite CONRAD's perfectly legitimate son, Conrad, who was only two years old. This poor lad was eventually beheaded at Naples in 1268.)

MANFRED (1232-1266), reigned 1258-1266. He was FREDERICK's illegitimate son, who had the throne secured for him only to be defeated by Charles of Anjou and killed by his agency. He was the last Hohenstauffen.

CHARLES OF ANJOU (1226-1285), reigned 1266-1282. The son of LOUIS VIII of France, he was the first and last of the Angevin dynasty of Naples. The Pope having given him the island, Charles lost it again during an uprising now called the *Sicilian Vespers*. He was deposed.

PETER I (1236-1285), reigned 1282-1285. MANFRED's son-in-law, he was offered the crown after the *Sicilian Vespers* affair. He was the first Aragon of the Sicilian dynasty.

JAMES (1260-1327), reigned 1285-1295. He became JAMES II of Aragon.

FREDERICK II (1272-1337), reigned 1295-1337. The third son of PETER, he was elected king by the Sicilian Parliament.

PETER II (died 1342), FREDERICK's son, reigned 1337-1342.

LOUIS (1338-1355), PETER's son, reigned 1342-1355.

FREDERICK III, 'The Simple' (1341-1377), reigned 1355-1377. He was another of PETER's sons.

MARY (died 1402), reigned 1377-1402. She was FREDERICK's (not so simple) daughter, who reigned alone until 1391 and then with her husband.

MARTIN I (died 1409), reigned 1402-1409. He ruled jointly with his wife, MARY, until her death in 1402 and then alone for a further seven years.

MARTIN II (died 1410), reigned 1409-1410. Rather confusingly, Martin II was MARTIN I's *father*. He was also MARTIN II of Aragon. A two-year interregnum followed his rule.

FERDINAND I, 'The Just' (1373-1416), reigned 1412-1416. He was also FERDINAND of Aragon and a nephew of MARTIN II. Since the kingdom was now under Spanish rule, he sent the Infante Don Juan to govern the island.

ALFONSO (1385-1458), reigned 1416-1458. The son of FERDINAND, he recalled the Infante and despatched a Viceroy, so beginning a long and usually unhappy history of viceregal government.

JOHN (1397-1479), reigned 1458-1460. He was ALFONSO's brother and King of Aragon as well. He ceded Sicily to FERDINAND.

FERDINAND II, 'The Catholic' (1452-1516), reigned 1460-1516. In 1500, the Treaty of Granada divided the kingdom between Ferdinand and LOUIS XII of France. Three years later the French were expelled and Spain had total power over the island until 1707. He was also Ferdinand V of Castile.

JOANNA (1479-1555), reigned 1516-1555. Called *La Loca* 'The Mad', of Spain, she married PHILIP I in 1496. She was the last of the House of Trastamara. Having, in effect, been certified mad in 1506, Philip was given full powers to act for her.

The Habsburg Kings of Spain then reigned for nearly 200 years. Details of the following five monarchs will be found under Spain. The dates are dates of accession only.

CHARLES I, 1516
PHILIP II, 1556
PHILIP III, 1598
PHILIP IV, 1621
CHARLES II, 1665

PHILIP V of Spain pressed his claims to Sicily from 1700 until 1735, though he continued a (broken) Spanish reign until 1746. He was a Bourbon king.

JOSEPH (1678-1711), reigned 1707-1711. He was Archduke of Austria, a Habsburg, King of Germany and Hungary and Emperor of the Holy Roman Empire.

CHARLES III (1685-1740), reigned 1711-1713. He was JOSEPH's brother and holder of the same titles.

VICTOR AMADEUS, of Savoy (1666-1732), reigned 1713-1718. By a complicated arrangement, under the *Treaty of Utrecht* he 'exchanged' Savoy for Sicily, then swapped Sicily for Sardinia in August 1718.

CHARLES III reigned again 1718-1735, during which time Naples was reunited with Sicily. He was the last Habsburg.

CHARLES IV (1716-1788), reigned 1735-1759. This Charles was a Bourbon Spaniard and also CHARLES III of Spain. Austria withdrew and eventually the Kingdom of the Two Sicilies came into being, under the control of Charles's son.

FERDINAND I (1751-1825), reigned 1759-1825. The first King of the Two Sicilies, he gave way to the Bonapartes in 1806. Details of these two Frenchmen can be found under Naples. After the fall of MURAT in 1815, Ferdinand came back to 'both thrones' for ten years.

FRANCIS I (1777-1830), reigned 1825-1830. The son of FERDINAND, he was born in Naples and died there.

FERDINAND II (1810-1859), reigned 1830-1859. He was the king whom Gladstone, the British Prime Minister, called 'The Negation of God'. Coarse, cruel and debauched, his fondness for allowing his troops the indiscriminate use of bombs to suppress the few small voices which objected to his tyrannical regime, caused him to be labelled 'Bomba'. Much to everyone's surprise, after the Revolt of 1848, he pardoned most of the ringleaders of the uprising.

FRANCIS II (1836–1894), reigned 1859–1860. Sicily was annexed by Italy in 1860, but this son of FERDINAND held out against Garibaldi's 'Thousand' troops, even though the King's battles and his realm were lost. He died in exile in Austria and Sicily became part of united Italy.

SPAIN

The marriage of ISABELLA of Castile to FERDINAND of Aragon and the subsequent conquest of Granada, at the end of the fifteenth century, created a united country, with the exception of Navarre, which was included later. The first king of virtually all Spain was of the House of Trastamara. The house ruled until the Habsburgs came to the throne in 1504. They stayed until 1700, when the Bourbons arrived. The line remained, despite interruptions from the Emperor NAPOLEON and the dictator Franco. (Rulers of parts of Spain have been covered under Aragon, Leon and Asturias, Leon and Castile and Navarre.)

Capital *MADRID*; currency *peseta*

FERDINAND V (1452–1516), reigned 1479–1516. The son of JOHN II of Aragon, he was also King of Naples, FERDINAND II of Aragon and King of Castile. He married ISABELLA, the sister of King HENRY IV of Leon and Castile, in October 1469. On the death of the feeble King Henry in 1474, the Kingdoms of Castile and Aragon were united.

ISABELLA I (1451–1504), reigned 1474–1504. The wife of FERDINAND, like her husband, she was known as 'The Catholic'. She and her confessor, Ximenes, spread Catholicism forcibly and expelled some Spanish Jews. It was FERDINAND and she who financed Christopher Columbus in 1491.

JOANNA, *La Loca* (1479–1555), reigned 1504–1516. The daughter of FERDINAND and ISABELLA, she married Archduke Philip of Austria in 1496. A passionate woman, given to jealous fits over her husband's (often unfaithful) behaviour, she became insane in about 1502. On the death of her mother, PHILIP ruled for her. He died in September 1506, having been officially given full royal power only the month before, and Joanna, now completely deranged, refused to leave his corpse for days. FERDINAND then took over the throne. He died in 1516.

CHARLES I (1500-1556), reigned 1516-1555. JOANNA's son (who did not, luckily, inherit her mental problems) was also Emperor of Germany and, in his time, probably the most powerful man in Europe. Despite vast territories both in Europe and the 'New World', Charles expressed a preference for his Flemish subjects and only spent seventeen of the forty years of his reign actually in Spain. Tired of power, partly disillusioned, he abdicated and retired to a monastery.

PHILIP II (1527-1598), reigned 1556-1598. He was the son of CHARLES I and King of Portugal. He is best remembered as the beloved husband of MARY Tudor, of England. He was hated by the English and used as a sort of 'frightener', in both English and Dutch nurseries, to scare young children into behaving. Philip was not as black as he was painted, but his grandiose thinking led Spain along the perilous path to bankruptcy.

PHILIP III (1578-1621), reigned 1598-1621. He was the son of PHILIP II, by his fourth and final wife, Anne of Austria. During his reign, the Moors (*Moriscos*) were finally cleared from Spain's mainland.

PHILIP IV (1605-1665), reigned 1621-1665. Despite the ability of his minister, Olivares, the young king could only watch his country slide further downhill. A revolt in Catalonia gave Portugal the chance to re-establish its independence.

CHARLES II (1661-1700), reigned 1665-1700. He was the son of PHILIP IV and the last of the Habsburgs. His childlessness precipitated the *War of the Spanish Succession*.

PHILIP V (1683-1746), reigned 1700-1746. The first Bourbon, he was the grandson of LOUIS XIV of France. He lost Gibraltar in 1704 and, by the *Treaty of Utrecht*, Spain was obliged to give away the Spanish Netherlands, Sicily and Naples. He abdicated in favour of his son LOUIS in January 1746, but the boy, only seventeen years old, died on September 6. Philip took back the crown for 22 more years.

FERDINAND VI, 'The Wise' (1712-1759), reigned 1746-1759. He married the dominant Barbara of Portugal, who died in 1758 and he followed her, insane, less than two years later.

CHARLES III (1716-1788), reigned 1759-1788. The brother of FERDINAND and fifth son of PHILIP V, he was King of the Two Sicilies, King of Naples and Duke of Parma. He built the Prado, in Madrid. His efforts to reform the Church in Spain, resulted in the expulsion of the Jesuits.

CHARLES IV (1748-1819), reigned 1788-1808. He was the second son of CHARLES III and had a greater affinity to painters than ships. Thus, he was Goya's patron, but failed to prevent the English, under Nelson, destroying his fleet at Trafalgar, in 1805. His wife, Maria Louisa, ran rings around him and was flauntingly faithless with the politician, Godoy. It was Godoy's despicable peace with France that eventually led to Charles's first abdication in March, 1808. After less than three months, during which the hapless twenty-four-year-old FERDINAND VII was on the throne, Charles restored himself. He stayed until the end of 1808, when he handed over to NAPOLEON.

JOSEPH BONAPARTE (1768-1844), reigned 1808-1813.

NAPOLEON's elder brother, he was also King of Naples. He made little impression on Spain and was deposed.

FERDINAND VII (1784-1833), 1813-1833. The eldest (surviving) son of CHARLES IV, he had been a prisoner of the French, an experience which coloured his subsequent behaviour. He ruled despotically and foolishly, losing the South American colonies in 1820. From none of his four wives could he produce a son, so he changed the laws of succession in order that his daughter, ISABELLA II, could become Queen Regnant. Such legislative manipulation infuriated his brother Charles and the *Carlist Wars* began.

ISABELLA II (1830-1904), reigned 1833-1868. The daughter of FERDINAND, she was the unwitting cause of the *Carlist Wars*. Though only thirteen, she assumed control of the Government in 1843. As if matters were not already difficult enough for her, in 1846 she married her half-witted, impotent cousin, Don Francisco de Bourbon and revolt raised its ugly head. She was deposed in a coup, led by an ex-lover, Serrano.

AMADEUS (1820-1890), reigned 1870-1873. His rule followed a two-year regency. The second son of VICTOR EMANUEL II of Italy, he was elected King of Spain. Kingship was not to his liking and he abdicated as soon as he could.

A republic was declared in February 1873 only to end, five presidents later, in December 1874.

ALFONSO XII (1857-1885), reigned 1874-1885. He was ISABELLA's son, but by whom? He died without an heir.

MARIA CHRISTINA (1858-1929), reigned 1885-1886. Three months pregnant by ALFONSO when he died, she filled in as a 'child-bearing Regent' for six months. She was tactful and politically capable. Her son was born into a much more stable Spain on May 17, 1886.

ALFONSO XIII (1886-1941) reigned 1886-1931. He was a true courtier and obviously something of a curiosity. (The last time a child had been *born* a king was in 1316 in France, when LOUIS X died five months before his short-lived son, JOHN, was born.) Alfonso's life was one of nervous excitement. In 1906, he married Queen Victoria's granddaughter, Princess Ena of Battenberg. They narrowly escaped being killed when a bomb, intended for the royal couple, killed the horses drawing the bridal carriage away from the church after the wedding ceremony. The assassination attempt was only one of several. In 1931, civil war threatened when the Republicans gained a majority. Alfonso left the country, though he refused to abdicate. (General Franco, who became the Spanish dictator in October 1936, reinstated the king as a 'private citizen' and restored his confiscated property.) He never went back to Spain alive; he died in Rome in February 1941.

JUAN CARLOS (born 1938), his reign began in 1975. He was ALFONSO XIII's grandson and restored after Franco's death (though Spain was theoretically restored as a kingdom in March 1947). Juan Carlos was created the Prince of Spain in 1961 and officially declared heir to the throne in 1971. He married Sophia, daughter of King PAUL of Greece and their third child, Philip, born in 1968, is heir to the throne.

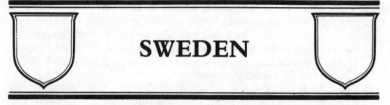

SWEDEN

Written Swedish history can only be relied on from the tenth century AD, though saga and legend provide a colourful past record long before then. The Skoldung family, followed by the Folkungs in the mid-thirteenth century, occupied the throne, which was united with both Denmark and Norway by Queen MARGARET of Denmark in 1387. Power ebbed and flowed until revolt brought the Vasa family to the top of the tree and they created a powerful Sweden. The Wittelsbachs, who succeeded them, suffered badly and, in 1751, a weakened country came under the Oldenburgs. They lasted until 1818, when the ex-Marshall Bernadotte, a Frenchman who had been chosen as Crown Prince, became KARL XIV. His family still occupies the throne.

Capital *STOCKHOLM*; currency *krona*

OLAF SKOTKONUNG, 'The Infant' (died 1022), reigned 995-1022. Prior to Olaf, the kings had been styled 'Kings of Upsal'. He united the Swedes with the Goths and during his reign Christianity was spread through the newly-created Swedish kingdom.

ANUND JAKOB (died 1050), the son of Olaf, he reigned 1022-1050.

EMUND (died 1060), reigned 1050-1060. ANUND's half-brother, called 'The Old', he actually *was* older than Anund.

STENKIL RAGNVALDSON (died 1066), reigned 1060-1066. He was the son-in-law of EDMUND and a noble from Vastergotland. An interregnum, lasting until 1078, followed.

HALSTEN (died 1099), reigned 1079-1099. STENKIL's son, he was a co-ruler with INGE and possibly with BLOT SVEN.

INGE I (died 1112), reigned 1080-1112. Until 1099, with one short break, he shared the throne with his brother, HALSTEN. He was overthrown by BLOT SVEN, but later killed him and returned to the throne.

BLOT SVEN (died 1083), reigned 1081-1083. He was probably the brother-in-law of INGE, whom he overthrew when leading a recrudescence of pagan feeling against national Christianity.

PHILIP (died 1118), reigned 1112-1118. INGE's son, he co-ruled with his brother.

INGE II (1125), reigned 1112-1125. He shared the throne with PHILIP.

MAGNUS I (died 1134), reigned 1129-1134. He was the son of NIELS of

Denmark by a daughter of INGE I.

SVERKER I (died 1156), reigned 1134-1156. He consolidated the union between Goths and Swedes, begun by OLAF some 150 years before. Sverker was one step out of the family lineage, being BLOT SVEN's grandson.

ERIC IX, St Eric (died 1160), reigned 1156-1160. He tried to convert Finland to Christianity, but only succeeded in getting himself killed at Upsala by an invading Danish prince leading a band of Swedish rebels. His memory was perpetuated by his son, Eric, and he was canonized, becoming Sweden's patron saint. His saintly and kingly record both leave room for doubt.

MAGNUS II (died 1161), the great-grandson of INGE I, reigned 1160-1161.

KARL VII (died 1167), reigned 1161-1167. The son of SVERKER I, he was killed by his cousin KNUT I.

KNUT I, Ericssen (died 1196), reigned 1176-1196. He was the first of three kings of the House of Jedvardssen.

SVERKER II (died 1210), reigned 1196-1208. The son of KARL VII, he was deposed by KNUT's son ERIC.

ERIK X (died 1216), son of KNUT I, reigned 1208-1216.

JOHN I, Sverkerssen (died 1229), reigned 1216-1222. Like his father, SVERKER II, he was deposed.

ERIK XI (died 1250), reigned 1222-1250. The last of the Jedvardssens, he was deposed by Knut II (of very doubtful origin) in 1229. He was returned to the throne in 1234.

VALDEMAR I (1238-1302), reigned 1250-1275. He was the son of ERIC XI's sister and, as he was only twelve years old on his accession, his father, Birger Jarl, ruled for him. Birger was one of the great medieval statesmen and has often been called 'King' by historians, though he never assumed the title. He founded Stockholm and ruled Sweden autocratically. His lasting achievements were the measures he instituted which led the way to the abolishment of serfdom. MAGNUS, who deposed Valdemar, extended Birger's successes.

MAGNUS III, Ladulas (1240-1290), reigned 1275-1290. He was the brother of VALDEMAR, whom he deposed. He set about the slightly risky process of creating a number of almost independent Swedish duchies.

BIRGER (1280-1321), reigned 1290-1318. He was the son of MAGNUS and so grandson of Birger Jarl, but he was not 'Birger II' as he has sometimes been erroneously styled. He was usurped by his brothers Erik and Valdemar, though they never formally assumed kingship.

MAGNUS IV, *Smek* (1316-1374), reigned 1319-1365. The nephew of BIRGER, he had an 'on-off' reign until his deposition in 1365. In 1356 he was joined by ERIK XII, who co-ruled with him for two years. He was also MAGNUS VII of Norway.

ERIK XII (1339-1359), reigned 1356-1359. He co-ruled with his father, MAGNUS, whom he forced into co-operation.

ALBERT OF MECKLENBURG (1340-1412), reigned 1365-1389. He was the son of a sister of MAGNUS IV. He was put up, as a puppet king, by a group of nobles. They soon discovered the puppet did not respond to their manipulation, but had a mind of his own. He was deposed by the now wiser group of nobles and replaced by Queen MARGARET of Denmark.

The Danish monarchs ruled over Sweden until 1523. The list which follows shows their dates of accession only and more detail will be found under Denmark.

MARGARET, 1389 (1387 in Norway)
ERIC XIII, 1412
CHRISTOPHER, 1440
CHARLES VIII, 1448, deposed
CHRISTIAN I, 1457
CHARLES VIII resumed the throne in 1464.
Interregnum, 1470, under a regent, Sten Sture, the Elder
JOHN II, 1497, deposed
Interregnum, 1501, under three different Stures
CHRISTIAN II, 1520, deposed

GUSTAV I (1496-1560), reigned 1523-1560. A man who had been brought up to mistrust the Danes and all things Danish, he was taken prisoner to Denmark by King CHRISTIAN in 1516. He returned to his native land and, between 1521-1523, proceeded to expel the Danes. He was crowned, as an elected king, on June 6, 1523. He broke with the *Hanseatic League* and, despite a stern, nearly cruel style of kingship, created a strong Swedish monarchy. He was an imposing figure with '...a ruddy countenance...and a body as fitly and well proportioned as any painter could have painted it'.

ERIC XIV (1533-1577), reigned 1560-1568. He was GUSTAV's elder son (by one of his three marriages) and the second king of the Vasa dynasty. Eric disposed of the Stures, quarrelled with his half-brothers and made his mistress Queen Consort. Not popular (understandably) he was deposed, when it was alleged he was insane. He was probably as sane as his accusers.

JOHN III (1537-1592), reigned 1568-1592. The brother of ERIC XIV, he was theologically inclined but dynastically weak.

SIGISMUND (1566-1637), reigned 1592-1599. The son of JOHN III, he became a Catholic and was elected King of Poland. He was deposed.

CHARLES IX (1550-1611), JOHN's brother, reigned 1599-1611. Having deposed his nephew SIGISMUND, Charles, by using unpopular means, began to bring the country back into line with his Calvinistic views. He also marched the Swedish army as far as Moscow and the Russian throne was offered to his son, GUSTAV. He attacked Poland, Denmark and Finland, leaving three nicely simmering wars for his son to cope with when, unmourned, he died aged 61.

GUSTAV ADOLF II (1594-1632), reigned 1611-1632. The son of CHARLES IX, he was a brilliant general, a fluent Latinist and was possessed with foresight. His involvement in the *Thirty Years War* had a long-term non-military consquence: Protestantism was unshakeably established in North Germany. He created a small empire for Sweden and opportunities for the country it did not have the ability to exploit. He was killed fighting the Germans at the *Battle of Lutzen*.

CHRISTINA (1626-1689), reigned 1632-1654. She was only six when her father GUSTAV was killed and the fine Swedish statesman, Axel Oxenstierna, acted as Regent. When Christina was allowed to act for herself, she advanced Swedish awareness of culture and depleted the treasury. Illegally, she became a Catholic and was averse to any attentions paid by potential suitors. 'Her countenance was sprightly, but somewhat pale...and though her person was of smaller size, yet her mien and carriage was very noble.' She refused to marry, abdicated and lived in exile in Rome, where Scarlatti and Bernini were amongst her friends.

CHARLES X (1622-1660), reigned 1654-1660. Prince Carl of the Palatinate, he was grandson of CHARLES IX. His short reign was warlike, but otherwise undramatic.

CHARLES XI (1655-1697), reigned 1660-1697. His widowed mother was one of six regents. He restored the armed forces and reduced the national debt from about 44 million to 15 million *thalers*.

CHARLES XII (1682-1718), reigned 1697-1718. He was declared of age when only fifteen, although 'addicted to wild pranks and perilous sports'. He was, despite such high spirits, a great patriot. He lost the *Battle of Poltava* to the Russians (having defeated Poland) and was forced into exile from 1709-1714. He was killed by a bullet whilst in Norway looking for allies to help him fight back against Russian-aided Denmark.

ULRIKA (1688-1741), reigned 1718-1720. CHARLES's sister and married to Frederick of Hesse Cassel, she was elected to the throne. Two years later, she abdicated and passed the crown to her husband.

FREDERICK (1676-1751), reigned 1720-1751. When he acquired the throne, upon his wife, ULRIKE's, abdication, he found the country to be bankrupt.

ADOLF FREDERICK (born 1710), reigned 1751-1771. The Prince of Holstein-Gottorp, he was elected king as a result of pressure from a political group called *The Hats*. His wife wore the breeches, however.

GUSTAV III (1746-1792), reigned 1771-1792. During his reign the government 'nationalised' the distillation of alcohol, a pastime which had previously been a source of pleasure and profit to the peasants. His mother tried to interfere during Gustav's reign as she had done during his father, ADOLF's. The king was murdered at an Opera House Ball in Stockholm, by an army captain.

GUSTAV IV (1772-1837), reigned 1792-1809. He was the son of GUSTAV III. His stubbornness led to an army coup in March 1809. The king was taken prisoner and forced to abdicate.

CHARLES VIII (1748-1818), reigned 1809-1818. An uncle of GUSTAV IV, he came to the throne after a three-month interregnum. Charles was childless and in 1810 he 'adopted' a French Marshal, Count Jean-Baptiste Bernadotte, who was 47 years old. Bernadotte was a shrewd man and, in any case, Sweden wished to keep the friendship of the all-victorious NAPOLEON. Bernadotte changed his name to

Charles John and became the Crown Prince. A special ordinance was passed so that he became heir to the throne.

CHARLES XIV (1763-1844), reigned 1818-1844. He was the first Bernadotte. He dropped all Swedish claims to Finland and managed to acquire Norway as compensation. Considering he never learned to speak Swedish, Charles/Bernadotte ruled the country well, if a little cautiously.

OSCAR I (1799-1859), reigned 1844-1859. A more gifted, if less strong-minded man than his father, CHARLES, Oscar pursued a number of lines of small reforms. During his reign, the decision to build the main railway lines as nationalised concerns, was taken.

CHARLES XV, (1826-1972), reigned 1859-1872. He had been virtually ruler of the country for the last two years of his father, OSCAR's reign.

OSCAR II (1829-1907), reigned 1872-1907. The third son of OSCAR I, he was a writer and a musician who made his feelings about his dual kingdom of Sweden and Norway perfectly clear. Trouble brewed and Oscar finally laid down his Norwegian crown on October 26, 1905.

GUSTAV V (1858-1950), reigned 1907-1950. The dignified and retiring eldest son of OSCAR II, he kept Sweden neutral during both the World Wars.

GUSTAV VI, Adolf (1882-1973), reigned 1950-1973. He was an archaeologist, an expert on porcelain and the last Swedish king to have any real constitutional power.

CARL XVI, Gustav (born 1946), his reign began in 1973. The grandson of GUSTAV VI, he married a commoner, Fraülein Renate Sommerlath, in 1976. They have three children.

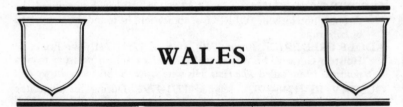

WALES

After the Romans withdrew from Britain (a gradual evacuation, completed by AD 436) a number of Welsh principalities were formed, which were briefly united by Rhodri in the ninth century. He was killed by the Angles in 878. The Norman kings never really subdued Wales, but finally, in 1542, the country was formally joined with England.

Capital (today) *CARDIFF*

LLYWELYN AP SEISYLL (died 1023), reigned 999-1023. He was King of Deheubarth and great-grandson of Anarawd, who had been Prince of Gwynedd 878-916. Gwynedd was the northern 'kingdom' of the country and embraced the region of Snowdonia.

RHYDDERCH AB IESTYN (died 1033), reigned 1023-1033. He was also King of Deheubarth.

IAGO AB IDWAL (died 1039), reigned 1033–1039. He was the great-grandson of Idwal Foel, who had been Prince of Gwynedd after Anarawd. Iago's own men split his head open with an axe.

GRUFFYDD AP LLYWELYN (died 1063), reigned 1039–1063. The son of LLYWELYN, he became King of All Wales after his victory at the battle of Tywi. He, too, was murdered.

BLEDDYN AP CYFYN (died 1075), reigned 1063–1075. He was a half-brother to GRUFFYDD and a grandson, through a daughter, to Maredudd of Gwynedd (d.999).

TRAHAERN AP CARADOG (died 1081), reigned 1075–1081. He was a cousin of BLEDDYN and yet another victim of a murderous plot.

GRUFFYDD AP CYNAN (1055–1137), reigned 1081–1137. The ruler of north Wales, he spent the first twelve years of his reign imprisoned in England by order of King WILLIAM, 'The Conqueror'. His imprisonment continued during the first six years of the reign of WILLIAM, 'Rufus'. He was succeeded by his sons, the younger one first, but they were styled as princes not kings.

WESTPHALIA

This kingdom was created by the Emperor NAPOLEON in 1807. It formed nearly all Hesse-Cassel, all Brunswick and large parts of Prussia, Hannover and Saxony. It ceased to exist in 1813, after the battle of Leipsic.

Capital *CASSEL*

JEROME BONAPARTE (1784–1860), reigned 1807–1813. Like his elder brother, NAPOLEON, Jerome was born in Ajaccio, Corsica. He was the most dissolute of the Emperor's dissolute bunch of siblings. He married a Miss Elizabeth Patterson of Baltimore in 1803 but, having been created king of a puppet kingdom, he took Princess Catherine of Wurttemberg as his consort. After he fled in 1813, he married Giustina Pecori – for her money.

WURTTEMBERG

It was formerly called Wirtemberg. A southern German kingdom and a state in the Empire, it was bounded by Bavaria on three sides and Lake Constance in the south. Having been ruled by the same family for over 700 years, it became a kingdom on December 26, 1805.

Capital *STUTTGART*

FREDERICK I (1754–1816), reigned 1805–1816. Having become Duke Frederick II when his father died in 1797, he was elector in 1803 and king two years later. As a second wife, he took Charlotte, the Princess Royal, daughter of GEORGE III of Great Britain. He formed an advantageous alliance with NAPOLEON and gained further territory. However, in 1813, he deserted the Emperor and joined the Allies.

WILLIAM I (1781–1864), reigned 1816–1864. The son of FREDERICK (by his first wife) William abolished serfdom in the kingdom. In 1862 he became the oldest living sovereign, dying two years later, four months before his eighty-third birthday.

CHARLES (1823–1891), reigned 1864–1891. WILLIAM's only son, he saw his country absorbed by the German Empire only seven years after he came to the throne. Despite the 'takeover', Wurttemberg controlled a number of its own services autonomously.

WILLIAM II (1848–1921), reigned 1891–1918. He was FREDERICK's great-grandson. The constitution was revised in 1906, but the revolution broke out soon after the First World War and William resigned. A republican constitution was adopted in 1919.

YUGOSLAVIA

The country became a republic in November 1945. It is made up of the Socialist Republics of Serbia, Croatia, Slovenia, Montenegro, Bosnia and Herzegovina, Macedonia. It is one of the more 'free-thinking' satellite countries of the communist bloc.

Capital *BELGRADE* currency *dinar*

PETER I (1844–1921), reigned 1918–1921. The son of Alexander, Prince of Serbia, Peter lived in exile from 1858. He joined the French army in 1870 and later fought against the Turks under the name of Mrkonjić. He was elected the first King of the Serbs, Croats and Slovenes, having been King of Serbia since 1903. Ill health required him to entrust the Crown Prince with the regency and he died in retirement at Topola.

ALEXANDER I (1888–1934), reigned 1921–1934. Dissident elements within the kingdom forced him to adopt a dictatorial role. The unpopularity this created, led to his assassination in Marseilles by a gunman hired by a secret society of Croatian nationals. His Queen, Marie, was the great-granddaughter of Queen VICTORIA of Great Britain.

PETER II (1923–1970) reigned 1934–1945. He was exiled when Tito came to power and left his country promising to '...liberate Yugo-Slavia from tyranny...'. This, of course, he could not do. Eventually he moved to the United States and died in Denver, Colorado. (His son, born in 1945, uses the family name of Karageorgevitch. Until 1984, he was the fifty-fourth in line of succession to the throne of Great Britain.)

Conversion Table

Chronology of Monarchs

The names of monarchs used in the book showing their national variants

Name as in Text	Denmark	France	Germany	Hungary	Italy
ALBERT			Albrecht		
ALEXANDER					
ALFONSO			Alfons		
AMADEUS					
ANDREW				Andras	
ANTHONY					
BEATRICE					
BLANCHE					
BOLESLAV					
CATHERINE					
CHARLES			Carl/Karl		Carlo
CHRISTIAN					
CHRISTOPHER					
CONRAD			Konrad		Corrado
CONSTANTINE					
CONSTANTINE TICH					
EDWARD					
ELEANOR					
ELIZABETH					
ERIK					
ERNEST-AUGUSTUS					
FEODOR					
FERDINAND					Ferdinando
FRANCIS		François	Franz	Ferenc	Francesco
FRANCIS-PHOEBUS					
FREDERICK	Frederik		Friedrich		Federico
GEORGE			Georg		
HENRY		Henri	Heinrich		Enrico
INGE					
JEROME					
JAMES					Giacomo

Norway Sweden	Poland	Russia	Spain	Other variants
	Olbracht	Aleksandr		Albrekt (Bohemia) Alexandros (Greece) Afonso (Portugal)
			Amadeo	
				Anton (Saxony)
				Beatriz (Portugal) Blanca (Navarre)
	Boleslaw			
Carl/Karl Kristian Kristofer		Ekaterina	Carlos	
				Konstantinos (Greece) Konstantin Tikh (Bulgaria)
				Duarte (Portugal) Eléonore (Navarre)
Eirik		Elisaveta		
				Ernst-August (Hanover)
		Fyodor	Fernando	Ferrante (Naples)
				Francisco-Febo (Navarre)
Fredrik				
				Giorgios (Greece) Jiri (Bohemia) Georgi (Bulgaria)
			Enrique	Enrique (Portugal)
Ingi				
			Jaime	Hieronymus (Westphalia)

CONVERSION TABLE

Name as in Text	Denmark	France	Germany	Hungary	Italy
JOACHIM MURAT					
JOANNA					Giovanna
JOHN	Hans	Jean	Johann	János	Giovanni
JOSEPH				Jószef	Giuseppe
KASIMIR					
KNUT	Knud				
LADISLAS					
LADISLAV				Laszló	
LOTHAIR			Lothar		
LOUIS				Lajos	Lodovico
MANUEL					
MARGARET	Margarethe				
MARTIN					Martino
MATTHIAS				Mátyás	
MICHAEL					
MIESZKO					
NICHOLAS					
OLAF					
OSCAR					
OTHO					
PAUL					
PETER					Pierro
PHILIP		Philippe	Philipp		Filippo
PREMISLAS					
ROGER					Ruggiero
RUDOLPH		Rodolphe	Rodolf		
SEBASTIAN					
SIGISMUND					
STEPHEN				István	
SVERRE					
THEOBALD		Thibaut			
THEODORE			Theodor		
VACLAV			Wenzel		
VICTOR-EMMANUEL					Vittorio-Emanuele
VLADISLAV					
WILLIAM			Wilhelm		Guglielmo

Norway Sweden	Poland	Russia	Spain	Other variants
Johann	Jan		Juana Juan	Gioacchino Napoleone (Naples)
				João (Portugal) Ján (Bohemia)
Cnud	Kazimierz			
				Laslo (Naples) Vladislav (Bohemia)
	Ludwik		Luis	Ludvik (Bohemia)
Margrete/ Margaretha				Manoel (Portugal)
	Michal	Mikhail		Mihail (Bulgaria) Mihai (Romania)
	Mieczyslaw			
		Nikolai		
Olav/Olof Oskar				
				Othon (Greece)
		Pavel		Pavlos (Greece) Petur (Bulgaria)
			Felipe	Felippe (Portugal) Premysl (Bohemia)
				Sebastão (Portugal)
	Zygmunt Stefan			Stepan (Serbia)
Sverrir				
				Todor (Bulgaria)
	Waclaw			
	Wladyslaw			
				Willem (Netherlands)

List of monarchs from AD 978 to the present

KEY
HRE Emperor of the Holy Roman Empire
(J) Jointly, as a co-ruler
(AK) Anti-king
(LK) Last king of that kingdom
(LQ) Last queen of that kingdom

Date of Accession	Age at Accession	Monarch	Kingdom(s)	Date Reign Ended
978	10	ETHELRED	England	1016
983	3	OTTO	HRE	1002
986	–	SVEN	Denmark	1014
992	26	BOLESLAV I	Poland	1025
993	–	RUDOLPH III	Burgundy	1032
995	31	OLAF	Norway	1000
995	–	OLAF, Skotkonung	Sweden	1022
996	16	OTTO III	Germany, HRE	1002
996	26	ROBERT II	France	1031
999	–	LLYWELYN AP SEISYLL	Wales	1023
999	5	ALFONSO	Leon and Asturias	1028

999	Silvester II (Gebert) was elected Pope. He was popularly supposed to have introduced Arabic numerals into Europe and to have invented clocks.

Date of Accession	Age at Accession	Monarch	Kingdom(s)	Date Reign Ended
1000	8	SANCHO III	Navarre	1035
1000	23	STEPHEN I	Hungary	1038
1002	74	BRIAN, Boruma	Ireland	1014
1002	29	HENRY II	Germany, HRE	1024
1005	53	MALCOLM II	Scotland	1034
1014	–	HARALD II	Denmark	1019

1014	BRIAN, King of Ireland was killed at the *Battle of Clontarf* (April 23) whilst defeating the Danes.

Date of Accession	Age at Accession	Monarch	Kingdom(s)	Date Reign Ended
1014	–	MAEL, Sechmaill, II	Ireland	1022
1015	20	SAINT OLAF II	Norway	1030
1016	27	EDMUND	England	1016
1016	22	CANUTE	Norway, England, Denmark	1035
1022	–	ANUND JACOB	Sweden	1050
1023	–	RHYDDERCH AB IESTYN	Wales	1033
1024	34	CONRAD II	Germany, HRE	1039
1025	35	MIESZKO II	Poland	1034
1028	12	VERMUDO III	Leon and Asturias	1037
1031	20	HENRI I	France	1060
1033	–	IAGO AB IDWAL III	Wales	1039
1033	–	CONRAD II (LK)	Burgundy	1039
1034	18	KASIMIR I	Poland	1058
1034	–	DUNCAN I	Scotland	1040

Date of Accession	Age at Accession	Monarch	Kingdom(s)	Date Reign Ended
1035	11	MAGNUS I (J)	Norway	1047
1035	18	HAROLD	England, Denmark	1040
1035	–	GARCIA IV	Navarre	1054
1035	–	FERDINAND	Leon and Castile	1065
1035	–	RAMIRO I	Aragon	1063
1038	26	PETER	Hungary	1047
1039	22	HENRY III	Germany, HRE	1056
1039	–	GRUFFYDD AP LLYWELYN	Wales	1063
1040	–	MACBETH	Scotland	1057
1040	22	HARDICANUTE	England, Denmark	1042
1041	–	ABA	Hungary	1044
1042	38	EDWARD, 'The Confessor'	England	1066
1042	24	MAGNUS	Denmark, Norway	1047
1047	27	SVEN II	Denmark	1076
1047	34	ANDREW I	Hungary	1060
1047	15	HARALD III (J)	Norway	1066
1050	–	EMUND	Sweden	1060
1054	16	SANCHO IV	Navarre	1076
1056	6	HENRY IV	Germany, HRE	1106
1057	–	LULACH	Scotland	1058
1058	27	MALCOLM III	Scotland	1093
1058	19	BOLESLAV II	Poland	1079
1060	–	STENKIL	Sweden	1066
1060	44	BELA I	Hungary	1063
1060	7	PHILIPPE I	France	1108

1061		POLAND overran HUNGARY		

1063	38	BLEDDYN AP CYFYN (LK)	Wales	1075
1063	26	SANCHO IV	Aragon	1094
1064	12	SALOMON	Hungary	1074
1065	27	SANCHO II	Castile	1072

1066		The *Battle of Hastings* was fought on October 14. William of Normandy defeated and killed HAROLD II of England.		

1066	44	HAROLD II	England	1066
1066	39	WILLIAM I	England	1087
1066	18	MAGNUS (J)	Norway	1069
1066	16	OLAF III (J)	Norway	1093
1072	32	ALFONSO VI	Leon and Castile	1109
1072	–	TURLOUGH O'BRIEN	Ireland	1086
1074	–	GEZA I	Hungary	1077
1075	–	TRAHAERN AP CARADOG	Wales	1081
1076	39	SANCHO V	Navarre	1094
1076	–	HARALD III	Denmark	1080
1077	37	LADISLAS	Hungary	1095
1079	–	HALSTEN (J)	Sweden	1099
1079	36	VLADISLAV I	Poland	1102
1080	–	INGE I (J)	Sweden	1112
1080	–	KNUT IV	Denmark	1086

Date of Accession	Age at Accession	Monarch	Kingdom(s)	Date Re Ende
1081	26	GRUFFYDD AP CYNAN (LK)	Wales	1137
1081	–	BLOT SVEN	Sweden	1083
1081		WILLIAM, 'The Conqueror' of England invaded Wales.		
1086	–	MURTOUGH O'BRIEN	Ireland	1114
1086	–	OLAF I	Denmark	1095
1087	31	WILLIAM II	England	1100
1090	–	DONNELL O'LOUGHLIN	Ireland	1118
1093	33	DONALD III (J)	Scotland	1094
1093	20	MAGNUS III	Norway	1103
1093	–	CONRAD (AK)	HRE	1098
1094	34	DUNCAN II	Scotland	1094
1094	–	EDMUND (J)	Scotland	1097
1094	26	PEDRO	Navarre, Aragon	1104
1095	25	KOLOMAN	Hungary	1116
1095	39	ERIK I	Denmark	1103
1097	23	EDGAR	Scotland	1107
1099		On July 15, the First Crusade ended with the capture of Jerusalem and Godfrey of Bouillon was established as king.		
1100		The estimated population of Europe was 44 million.		
1100	32	HENRY I	England	1135
1102	17	BOLESLAV III	Poland	1138
1103	12	OLAF, Magnusson (J)	Norway	1115
1103	15	EYESTEIN I (J)	Norway	1122
1103	13	SIGURD I (J)	Norway	1130
1103	–	ERIK	Denmark	1104
1104	–	ALFONSO I	Navarre, Aragon	1134
1104	41	NIELS	Denmark	1134
1106	25	HENRY V	HRE, Germany	1125
1107	29	ALEXANDER I	Scotland	1124
1108	27	LOUIS VI	France	1137
1109	29	URRACA	Leon and Castile	1126
1112	–	PHILIP (J)	Sweden	1118
1112	18	ALFONSO I	Portugal	1185
1116	14	STEPHEN II	Hungary	1131
1118	–	INGE II	Sweden	1125
1118	–	TURLOUGH O'CONNOR	Ireland	1156
1124	44	SAINT DAVID	Scotland	1153
1125	50	LOTHAIR III	Germany, HRE	1137
1126	22	ALFONSO VII	Leon and Castile	1157
1129	–	MAGNUS I	Sweden	1134
1130	15	MAGNUS IV	Norway	1135
1130	35	ROGER II	Sicily, Naples	1154
1131	23	BELA II	Hungary	1141
1134	–	GARCIA V	Navarre	1150
1134	–	SVERKER I	Sweden	1156
1134	–	RAMIRO II	Aragon	1137

Date of Accession	Age at Accession	Monarch	Kingdom(s)	Date Reign Ended
1134	–	ERIK II	Denmark	1137
1135	32	HARALD IV	Norway	1136
1135	39	STEPHEN	England	1154
1136	2	SIGURD II (J)	Norway	1155
1136	1	INGE I (J)	Norway	1161
1137	–	ERIK III	Denmark	1147
1137	1	PETRONILLA	Aragon	1163
1137	17	LOUIS VII	France	1180
1138	45	CONRAD III	Germany, HRE	1152
1138	34	VLADISLAV II	Poland	1145
1141	10	GEZA II	Hungary	1161
1142	17	EYESTEIN II	Norway	1157
1146	19	BOLESLAV IV	Poland	1173
1147	–	SVEN III	Denmark	1157
1150	–	SANCHO VI	Navarre	1194
1152	29	FREDERICK I	Germany, HRE	1190

1152	Nicholas Breakspear, the Vatican Legate and to become the only English Pope (as Adrian IV) founded the Archbishopric of Trondheim in Norway.

Date of Accession	Age at Accession	Monarch	Kingdom(s)	Date Reign Ended
1153	11	MALCOLM IV	Scotland	1165
1154	34	WILLIAM I	Sicily	1166
1154	21	HENRY II	England	1189
1156	–	MURTOUGH	Ireland	1166
1156	–	SAINT ERIK IX	Sweden	1160

1156	Pope Adrian 'permitted' HENRY II of England to invade Ireland.

Date of Accession	Age at Accession	Monarch	Kingdom(s)	Date Reign Ended
1157	26	VALDEMAR	Denmark	1182
1157	23	SANCHO III	Castile	1158
1157	–	FERDINAND II	Leon	1188
1158	3	ALFONSO VIII	Leon and Castile	1188
1160	–	MAGNUS II	Sweden	1161
1161	–	KARL VII	Sweden	1167
1161	14	HAAKON II (J)	Norway	1162
1161	6	MAGNUS V	Norway	1184
1161	13	STEPHEN III	Hungary	1172
1163	11	ALFONSO II	Aragon	1196
1165	22	WILLIAM I	Scotland	1214
1166	12	WILLIAM II	Sicily	1189
1166	–	RORY O'CONNOR (LK)	Ireland	1186
1167	–	KNUT	Sweden	1196

1167	The *Lombard League* was formed. It consisted of the towns of Milan, Venice, Pavia and other important centres in northern Italy; uniting to resist the power of the German Emperor.

Date of Accession	Age at Accession	Monarch	Kingdom(s)	Date Reign Ended
1168	–	STEPHEN I, Nemanya	Serbia	1196
1172	22	BELA III	Hungary	1196
1173	47	MIESZKO III	Poland	1202

Date of Accession	Age at Accession	Monarch	Kingdom(s)	Date of End
1177	39	KASIMIR II	Poland	119
1180	15	PHILIPPE II	France	122
1181	19	KNUT VI	Denmark	120
1184	34	SVERRE	Norway	120
1185	31	SANCHO I	Portugal	1211
1187	–	ASEN	Bulgaria	119
1188	22	ALFONSO IX	Leon and Castile	123
1189	32	RICHARD I	England	1199
1189	–	TANCRED	Sicily	119
1190	25	HENRY VI	HRE, Germany	119
1191		On June 23, due to a total eclipse of the sun, stars were shining brightly over England at ten in the morning.		
1194	10	WILLIAM III	Sicily	1194
1194	29	HENRY VI	Sicily, HRE, Germany	1197
1194	9	LESZEK I	Poland	1227
1194	–	SANCHO VI	Navarre	1234
1196	–	STEPHEN II, Nemanya	Serbia	1227
1196	–	SVERKER II	Sweden	1208
1196	22	EMERIC	Hungary	1204
1196	–	PETER (J)	Bulgaria	1197
1196	22	PEDRO II	Aragon	1213
1197	–	KALOJAN	Bulgaria	1207
1197	4	FREDERICK I	Sicily	1250
1198	21	PHILIP	HRE, Germany	1208
1198	24	OTTO IV	HRE	1215
1198	48	PREMISLAS I	Bohemia	1230
1199	32	JOHN	England	1216
1200		The estimated population of Europe was about 58 million.		
1202	25	HAAKON III	Norway	1204
1202	32	VALDEMAR II (J)	Denmark	1241
1204	9	INGE II	Norway	1217
1204	5	LADISLAS III	Hungary	1205
1205	30	ANDREW II	Hungary	1235
1207	–	BORIL	Bulgaria	1218
1208	34	OTTO IV	Germany, HRE	1215
1208	–	ERIK X	Sweden	1216
1211	26	ALFONSO II	Portugal	1223
1212	18	FREDERICK II	Sicily, HRE, Germany	1250
1213	5	JAMES I	Aragon	1276
1214	16	ALEXANDER II	Scotland	1249
1214	11	HENRY I	Castile	1217
1215		On June 15, King JOHN of England was forced by his barons to sign the *Magna Carta* at Runnymede.		
1216	–	JOHN	Sweden	1222

Date of Accession	Age at Accession	Monarch	Kingdom(s)	Date Reign Ended
1216	9	HENRY III	England	1272
1217	3	HAAKON IV	Norway	1263
1217	17	FERDINAND III	Leon and Castile	1252
1218	–	IVAN ASEN II	Bulgaria	1241
1219		Gengis Khan invaded India. By the time he died in 1227, aged 65, his empire extended from the Black Sea to the Pacific.		
1222	–	ERIK XI	Sweden	1250
1223	14	SANCHO	Portugal	1248
1223	36	LOUIS VIII	France	1226
1226	11	LOUIS IX	France	1270
1227	–	STEPHEN III, Radoslav	Serbia	1234
1227	6	BOLESLAV V	Poland	1279
1230	25	VACLAV I	Bohemia	1253
1234	–	STEPHEN IV, Vladislav	Serbia	1243
1234	33	THEOBALD	Navarre	1253
1235	29	BELA IV	Hungary	1270
1241	25	ERIK IV (J)	Denmark	1250
1241	–	KOLOMAN	Bulgaria	1246
1243	–	STEPHEN I, Urosh	Serbia	1276
1246	42	HENRY RASPE	HRE	1247
1246	–	MICHAEL ASEN	Bulgaria	1257
1247	20	WILLIAM (AK)	HRE	1256
1248	38	ALFONSO III	Portugal	1279
1249	8	ALEXANDER III	Scotland	1286
1250	12	VALDEMAR I	Sweden	1275
1250	22	CONRAD IV	HRE, Germany, Sicily	1254
1250	32	ABEL	Denmark	1252
1252	31	ALFONSO X	Leon and Castile	1282
1252	33	CHRISTOPHER I	Denmark	1259
1253	46	THEOBALD II	Navarre	1270
1253	23	PREMISLAS II	Bohemia	1278
1257	–	CONSTANTINE TICH	Bulgaria	1277
1257	48	RICHARD	HRE	1272
1257	36	ALFONSO X	HRE, Leon and Castile	1273
1258	26	MANFRED	Sicily	1266
1259	10	ERIK V	Denmark	1286
1260		The capital city of Sweden, Stockholm was founded.		
1263	35	MAGNUS VI	Norway	1280
1265		In May, Dante Alighieri was born in Florence. He died in Ravenna fifty-six years later.		
1266	45	CHARLES of Anjou	Sicily, Naples	1282
1270	60	HENRY CRASSUS I	Navarre	1274
1270	41	STEPHEN V	Hungary	1272
1270	25	PHILIPPE III	France	1285

Date of Accession	Age at Accession	Monarch	Kingdom(s)	Date Reign Ended
1272	10	LADISLAS IV	Hungary	1290
1272	33	EDWARD I	England	1307
1273	55	RUDOLF	HRE, Germany	1291
1274	1	JOANNA (J)	Navarre	1305
1275	35	MAGNUS III	Sweden	1290
1276	40	PEDRO III	Aragon	1285
1276	33	STEPHEN VI, Dragutin	Serbia	1282
1278	7	VACLAV II	Bohemia, Poland	1305

1279		The University at Coimbra, Portugal, was founded.		

1279	–	LESZEK II	Poland	1289
1279	18	DIONYSIUS	Portugal	1325
1280	12	ERIK II	Norway	1299
1280	–	GEORGE, Terter	Bulgaria	1292
1282	–	STEPHEN II, Urosh Milutin	Serbia	1321
1282	46	PEDRO I	Aragon, Sicily	1285
1282	24	SANCHO IV	Leon and Castile	1295

1282		On March 30, the Sicilians, having become violently resentful toward the French citizens on the island, rose up (on Easter Monday) and slew an estimated 8,000 French residents in a massacre called the *Sicilian Vespers*.		

1285	20	ALFONSO III	Aragon	1291
1285	40	CHARLES II	Naples	1309
1285	15	JAMES	Sicily	1295
1285	17	PHILIPPE IV	France	1314
1286	4	MARGARET	Scotland	1290
1286	12	ERIK VI	Denmark	1319

1286		Konigsberg became the capital city of Prussia.		

1289	29	VLADISLAV I	Poland	1333
1290	10	BIRGER II	Sweden	1318
1290	–	PRZEMISLAV	Poland	1296
1290	26	ANDREW III	Hungary	1301
1291	31	JAMES	Aragon	1327

1291		The eighth (and last) Crusade ended with the Christians being driven out of Acre.		

1292	42	JOHN BALLIOL	Scotland	1296
1292	42	ADOLF	HRE, Germany	1298
1295	10	FERDINAND IV	Leon and Castile	1312
1295	23	FREDERICK II	Sicily	1337
1298	–	THEODORE	Bulgaria	1322
1298	48	ALBERT I	Germany, HRE	1308
1299	29	HAAKON V	Norway	1319

1300		The estimated population of Europe was about 79 million.		

1305	–	OTTO	Hungary	1309

Date of Accession	Age at Accession	Monarch	Kingdom(s)	Date Reign Ended
1305	26	VACLAV II	Bohemia, Poland	1306
1306	–	RUDOLPH	Bohemia	1307
1306	32	ROBERT I	Scotland	1329
1307		Declaration of Independence for Switzerland, freeing the country of Austrian rule. (Maximilian did not recognize the state until 1499.)		
1307	23	EDWARD II	England and Wales	1327
1307	–	HENRY	Bohemia	1310
1308	38	HENRY VII	HRE, Germany	1313
1309		Pope Clement V took up residence officially at Avignon in France.		
1309	34	ROBERT	Sicily, Hungary, Naples	1343
1310	14	JOHN	Bohemia	1346
1312	1	ALFONSO XI	Leon and Castile	1350
1314	28	FREDERICK (AK)	HRE	1330
1314	28	LUDWIG	HRE, Germany	1347
1314	25	LOUIS X	France, Navarre	1316
1316	0	JOHN I	France	1316
1316	23	PHILIPPE V	France, Navarre	1322
1319	3	MAGNUS VII (J)	Norway, Sweden	1365
1320	44	CHRISTOPHER II	Denmark	1326
1320		In Germany a monk, known as Bertholdus, was credited with having invented gunpowder.		
1321	–	STEPHEN III, Urosh	Serbia	1331
1322	–	GEORGE II	Bulgaria	1323
1322	28	CHARLES IV	France, Navarre	1328
1323	–	MICHAEL SHISHMAN	Bulgaria	1330
1325	34	ALFONSO IV	Portugal	1357
1327	15	EDWARD III	England and Wales	1377
1327	28	ALFONSO IV	Aragon	1336
1328	17	JOANNA	Navarre	1349
1328	35	PHILIPPE VI	France	1350
1329	5	DAVID II	Scotland	1371
1330	–	IVAN STEPHEN (J)	Bulgaria	1331
1331	–	IVAN ALEXANDER (J)	Bulgaria	1371
1331	23	STEPHEN Dushan	Serbia	1355
1332	–	EDWARD BALLIOL	Scotland	1346
1333	23	KASIMIR III	Poland	1370
1336	19	PEDRO IV	Aragon	1387
1337	–	PETER II	Sicily	1342
1340	20	VALDEMAR III	Denmark	1375
1340		The plague of the *Black Death* killed thousands in Italy.		
1342	4	LOUIS	Sicily	1355
1342	16	LOUIS	Hungary, Poland	1382
1343	3	HAAKON VI (J)	Norway, Sweden	1380

113

Date of Accession	Age at Accession	Monarch	Kingdom(s)	Date Reign Ended
1343	17	JOANNA	Naples	1382
1346	30	CHARLES I	Germany, Bohemia, HRE	1378
1347		On August 4, Edward III of England took Calais after a year's siege. The use of cannons by the English, was recorded for the first time.		
1347	33	CHARLES IV	Germany, HRE	1378
1349	45	GUNTHER (AK)	HRE	1349
1349	17	CHARLES II	Navarre	1387
1350		An English farm labourer at this time would have been paid about one penny (less than half a new penny) a day. This wage would double in the course of the next hundred years.		
1350	31	JOHN II	France	1364
1350	16	PEDRO	Leon and Castile	1369
1355	–	STEPHEN V, Urosh	Serbia	1371
1355	14	FREDERICK III	Sicily	1377
1356	17	ERIK XII (J)	Sweden	1359
1357	37	PEDRO	Portugal	1367
1364	27	CHARLES V	France	1380
1365	25	ALBERT	Sweden	1389
1366	33	HENRY II	Leon and Castile	1379
1367	22	FERDINAND I	Portugal	1383
1370	44	LOUIS	Poland, Hungary	1382
1371	6	IVAN SHISHMAN (J)	Bulgaria	1393
1371	55	ROBERT II	Scotland	1390
1375	5	OLAF II	Denmark, Norway	1387
1376	–	STEPHEN TVRTKO I	Bosnia	1391
1377	–	MARY (J)	Sicily	1402
1377	11	RICHARD II	England and Wales	1399
1378	17	VACLAV IV	HRE, Germany, Bohemia	1419
1379	21	JOHN I	Leon and Castile	1390
1380	–	OLAF IV	Norway, Denmark	1387
1380	12	CHARLES VI	France	1422
1382	37	CHARLES III	Naples, Hungary	1386
1382	12	MARY (J)	Hungary	1395
1383	–	BEATRICE	Portugal	1385
1384	11	JADWIGA (J)	Poland	1399
1385	28	JOHN I	Portugal	1433
1386	36	VLADISLAV II	Poland	1434
1386	9	LADISLAS	Naples	1414
1387	37	JOHN I	Aragon	1395
1387	35	MARGARET	Norway, Sweden, Denmark	1412
1387	19	SIGISMUND (J)	Hungary, Bohemia, HRE	1437
1387	26	CHARLES III	Navarre	1425

Date of Accession	Age at Accession	Monarch	Kingdom(s)	Date Reign Ended
1390	50	ROBERT III	Scotland	1406
1390	11	HENRY III	Leon and Castile	1406
1391	–	STEPHEN DABISHA	Bosnia	1395
1395	–	HELENA (R)	Bosnia	1398
1395	40	MARTIN (J)	Aragon, Sicily	1410
1398	18	STEPHEN OSTOJA	Bosnia	1418
1399	33	HENRY IV	England and Wales	1413
1400	–	FREDERICK	HRE	1400
1400	48	RUPERT III	HRE, Germany	1410
1402	–	MARTIN I	Sicily	1409
1404	–	STEPHEN TVRTKO II	Bosnia	1443
1406	1	JOHN II	Leon and Castile	1454
1406	12	JAMES I	Scotland	1437

1406	The plague killed more than 30,000 people in London. The population of Europe in 1400 has been estimated to have been about 60 million. Between 1347 and 1353 the plague, the *Black Death*, had killed between one quarter and one third of the people in Europe.

Date of Accession	Age at Accession	Monarch	Kingdom(s)	Date Reign Ended
1409	–	MARTIN II	Sicily	1410
1410	60	JOBST (AK)	HRE	1411
1412	31	ERIK VII	Denmark, Sweden, Norway	1438
1412	33	FERDINAND II	Aragon, Sicily	1416
1413	26	HENRY V	England and Wales	1422
1414	43	JOANNA	Naples	1435

1415	On October 25, Henry V of England defeated the French army at Agincourt; 10,000 French soldiers died.

Date of Accession	Age at Accession	Monarch	Kingdom(s)	Date Reign Ended
1416	31	ALFONSO V	Sicily, Aragon, Naples	1458
1418	–	OSTOJIC	Bosnia	1421
1419	41	SIGISMUND	HRE, Germany, Bohemia, Hungary	1437

1420	Tomas de Torquemada, the Spaniard, who organized the *Spanish Inquisition* was born. He died in 1498.

Date of Accession	Age at Accession	Monarch	Kingdom(s)	Date Reign Ended
1422	18	CHARLES VII	France	1461
1422	1	HENRY VI	England and Wales	1471
1425	20	BLANCHE (J)	Navarre	1441

1429	On April 29, Joan of Arc drove the English army out of Orléans leading the army of CHARLES II of France. She was burned at the stake by the English in May 1431.

Date of Accession	Age at Accession	Monarch	Kingdom(s)	Date Reign Ended
1433	42	EDWARD	Portugal	1438
1434	10	VLADISLAV III, Jagiellon	Poland, Hungary	1444
1437	40	ALBERT II	HRE, Hungary, Bohemia, Germany	1439
1437	7	JAMES II	Scotland	1460
1438	6	ALFONSO V	Portugal	1481

Date of Accession	Age at Accession	Monarch	Kingdom(s)	Date Re Ended
1440	25	FREDERICK III	Germany, HRE	1493
1440	22	CHRISTOPHER III	Norway, Denmark, Sweden	1448
1440	16	LADISLAV V	Bohemia, Hungary	1457
1440		Copenhagen became the capital city of Denmark.		
1441	44	JOHN II (J)	Navarre	1479
1443	–	STEPHEN THOMAS	Bosnia	1461
1447	20	KASIMIR IV	Poland	1492
1448	22	CHRISTIAN I	Denmark, Norway	1481
1452		On September 21, Girolamo Savanarola was born at Ferrara. Morally and religiously, but *not* theologically, Savanarola was per1aps the real initiator of the Reformation. He died in Florence in 1498.		
1454	19	HENRY IV (LK)	Leon and Castile	1474
1456		The Turks, under Mahomet II, conquered Athens and a large area of Greece.		
1458	61	JOHN II (LK)	Aragon, Sicily	1479
1458	38	GEORGE	Bohemia	1471
1458	15	MATTHIAS CORVINUS	Hungary, Bohemia	1490
1458	34	FERDINAND	Naples	1494
1460	8	FERDINAND V	Sicily, Castile	1516
1460	8	JAMES III	Scotland	1488
1461	20	EDWARD IV	England and Wales	1483
1461	38	LOUIS XI	France	1483
1461	–	STEPHEN (LK)	Bosnia	1463
1466		Athens was taken by the Venetians.		
1471	19	LADISLAV JAGIELLON	Bohemia, Hungary	1516
1474	23	ISABELLA	Spain	1504
1477		The fifty-five-year-old William Caxton published the first printed book in London, *The Dictes or Sayengis of the Philosophres*.		
1479	27	FERDINAND II	Aragon, Spain	1516
1479	–	FRANCIS-PHOEBUS	Navarre	1483
1479	–	ELEANOR de Foix	Navarre	1479
1481	26	JOHN II	Portugal	1495
1481	26	JOHN	Norway, Denmark, Sweden	1513
1483	13	EDWARD V	England and Wales	1483
1483	31	RICHARD III	England and Wales	1485
1483	–	CATHERINE (J)	Navarre	1512
1483	13	CHARLES VIII	France	1498
1485	28	HENRY VII	England and Wales	1509

Date of Accession	Age at Accession	Monarch	Kingdom(s)	Date Reign Ended
1487		The thirty-seven-year-old Bartolomeu Diaz, a navigator of King John of Portugal's court, discovered the Cape of Good Hope at the southernmost tip of Africa.		
1488	15	JAMES IV	Scotland	1513
1490	40	VLADISLAV II	Hungary, Bohemia	1516
1492	33	JOHN I	Poland	1501
1492		On April 17, Christopher Columbus set sail on the voyage during which he discovered West Indies.		
1493	34	MAXIMILIAN	HRE, Germany	1519
1494	46	ALFONSO II	Naples	1495
1495	26	MANUEL I	Portugal	1521
1495	28	FERDINAND II	Naples	1496
1496	44	FREDERICK IV	Naples	1501
1497		Vasco da Gama discovered the *Passage to India*.		
1498	36	LOUIS XII	France	1515
1500		The estimated population of Europe was about 81 million		
1500		In April Pedro Alvarez Cabral discovered Brazil and claimed the country on behalf of the King of Portugal.		
1501	40	ALEXANDER JAGIELLON	Poland	1506
1504	15	JOANNA (J)	Sicily, Spain, Naples	1555
1504		Leonardo da Vinci, aged 52, painted *The Mona Lisa*.		
1506	39	SIGISMUND I (J)	Poland	1548
1509	20	HENRY VIII	England and Wales	1547
1512	–	JOHN III	Navarre	1516
1513	1	JAMES V	Scotland	1542
1513	32	CHRISTIAN II	Norway, Denmark, Sweden	1523
1515	21	FRANCIS I	France	1547
1516	16	CHARLES I	Spain, Germany, HRE	1556
1516	13	HENRY II	Navarre	1555
1516	10	LOUIS II	Hungary, Bohemia	1526
1521	19	JOHN III	Portugal	1557
1521		On April 17, Martin Luther was excommunicated by the Diet at Worms, seat of the Holy Roman Empire.		
1523	27	GUSTAV I	Sweden	1560
1523	52	FREDERICK I	Denmark, Norway	1533
1526		The forty-eight-year-old Francisco Pizarro began to explore Peru. (He had been with Balboa in 1509, when the Pacific Ocean was discovered.)		

Date of Accession	Age at Accession	Monarch	Kingdom(s)	Date Reign Ended
1526	39	JOHN ZAPOLYA	Hungary	1540
1530	10	SIGISMUND (J)	Poland	1572
1533	3	IVAN	Russia	1584
1533	32	CHRISTIAN III	Denmark, Norway, Sweden	1559

1534		HENRY VIII of England parted company with the Church of Rome, establishing the Church of England.		

1540	37	FERDINAND I	Germany, Hungary	1563
1542	1 wk	MARY	Scotland	1567

1547		On October 9, Miguel de Cervantes, author of *Don Quixote*, was born. He died in Madrid in 1616.		

1547	28	HENRI II	France	1559
1547	10	EDWARD VI	England and Wales	1553

1551		The Protestant religion was officially established in Iceland. (The island had been Danish since 1397.)		

1553	16	Lady JANE Grey	England and Wales	1553

1553		On May 20, Sir Hugh Willoughby sailed from London to try and find a north-east passage to China.		

1554	38	MARY	England and Wales	1558
1555	17	JOANNA (LQ)	Navarre	1572
1556	39	PHILIP II	Spain, Portugal	1598
1556	53	FERDINAND I (LK)	Bohemia, Germany, HRE	1564
1557	3	SEBASTIAN	Portugal	1578
1558	25	ELIZABETH I	England and Wales	1603
1559	15	FRANCIS II	France	1560
1559	25	FREDERICK II	Norway, Denmark, Sweden	1588
1560	27	ERIK XIV	Sweden	1568
1560	10	CHARLES IX	France	1574

1564		April 23 (Saint George's Day) William Shakespeare was born at Stratford-upon-Avon and died there in 1616.		

1564	37	MAXIMILIAN II	Germany, Hungary, HRE	1576
1567	1	JAMES I	England and Scotland	1625
1568	31	JOHN III	Sweden	1592
1573	22	HENRI III	France, Poland	1589
1575	53	STEPHEN BATORY	Poland	1586
1576	24	RUDOLPH II	Germany, HRE, Hungary	1612

1578		King SEBASTIAN of Portugal was killed at the battle of Alcazar, in Morocco.		

1578	66	HENRY I	Portugal	1580

Date of Accession	Age at Accession	Monarch	Kingdom(s)	Date Reign Ended
1579		IVAN, 'The Terrible', of Russia sought to marry Queen ELIZABETH I of England.		
1582		Pope Gregory XIII published the *New Style Calendar* and October 5 became October 15. It was adopted by France, Italy, Spain, Denmark, Holland and Portugal the same year; by Germany and Switzerland in 1584 and Hungary in 1587. Great Britain did not come into line until 1751, when September 3 became September 14.		
1584	27	FEODOR I	Russia	1598
1587	21	SIGISMUND III	Poland, Sweden	1632
1588		Between July 21-27, the *Armada* of PHILIP of Spain was completely defeated by the English navy under Drake, Howard and Hawkins.		
1588	11	CHRISTIAN IV	Denmark, Sweden, Norway	1648
1589	36	HENRI IV	France	1610
1592	26	SIGISMUND	Sweden, Poland	1599
1594		On February 2, the composer, Giovanni Pierluigi da Palestrina, died in Rome, aged 70.		
1598	20	PHILIP III	Spain, Portugal	1621
1598	47	BORIS GODUNOV	Russia	1605
1599	49	CHARLES IX	Sweden	1611
1600		The estimated population of Europe was about 100 million.		
1605	16	FEODOR II	Russia	1605
1605	24	DMITRI II	Russia	1606
1606	54	VASILI IV	Russia	1610
1606		In March the Dutch discovered Australia. (Portugal had claimed discovery in 1601).		
1606		On July 15, Rembrandt van Rijn was born in Leyden. He died in Amsterdam in October 1669.		
1608	55	MATTHIAS II	Germany, Hungary, HRE	1619
1610		On January 8, the forty-five-year old Galileo Galilei discovered the planet Jupiter in his Paduan observatory.		
1610	9	LOUIS XIII	France	1643
1611	17	GUSTAV ADOLF II	Sweden	1623
1613	17	MICHAEL	Russia	1645
1619	41	FERDINAND II	Germany, Hungary, HRE	1637
1621	16	PHILIP IV	Spain, Portugal	1665

Date of Accession	Age at Accession	Monarch	Kingdom(s)	Date Reign Ended
1624		The Dutch founded Manhattan, now called New York.		
1625	25	CHARLES I	England, Wales and Scotland	1649
1628		Aged 50, William Harvey made public his 'discovery' of the circulation of the blood.		
1632	6	CHRISTINA	Sweden	1654
1632	37	VLADISLAV IV	Poland	1648
1634		Cardinal Richelieu organized the *Académie de France*.		
1637	29	FERDINAND III	Germany, Hungary, Bohemia, HRE	1657
1640	36	JOHN IV	Portugal	1656
1643	5	LOUIS XIV	France	1715
1645	16	ALEXEI	Russia	1676
1648	37	FREDERICK III	Denmark, Norway, Sweden	1670
1648	39	JOHN II	Poland	1648
1654	32	CHARLES X	Sweden	1660
1656	13	ALFONSO VI	Portugal	1667
1658	17	LEOPOLD I	Germany, Hungary, HRE	1705
1658		On September 3, Oliver Cromwell, Lord Protector and Head of State during the English Commonwealth, died. Soon after the country was beginning to show its monarchist sympathies again.		
1660	5	CHARLES XI	Sweden	1697
1660	30	CHARLES II	England, Wales and Scotland	1685
1662		Bombay was ceded to England as part of the dowry of Catherine of Braganza, when she married CHARLES II.		
1665	4	CHARLES II	Spain	1700
1669	31	MICHAEL WISNIOWIECKI	Poland	1673
1670	24	CHRISTIAN V	Denmark, Sweden, Norway	1699
1674	35	JOHN SOBIESKI	Poland	1696
1676	15	FEODOR III	Russia	1682
1682	16	IVAN V (J)	Russia	1696
1683	35	PEDRO	Portugal	1706
1685	52	JAMES II	England, Wales and Scotland	1688
1689	27	MARY II (J)	England, Wales and Scotland	1694
1689	39	WILLIAM III (J)	England, Wales and Scotland	1702

Date of Accession	Age at Accession	Monarch	Kingdom(s)	Date Reign Ended
1689		Warsaw became the seat of the Polish Government.		
1696	24	PETER I	Russia	1725
1697	15	CHARLES XII	Sweden	1718
1697	27	AUGUSTUS II	Poland	1733
1699	27	FREDERICK IV	Denmark, Sweden, Norway	1730
1700		The estimated population of Europe was about 120 million.		
1700	17	PHILIP V	Spain, Sicily	1746
1701	44	FREDERICK	Prussia	1713
1702	37	ANNE	Great Britain	1714
1703		On June 28, John Wesley, founder of the Methodist religion was born at Epworth, Lincolnshire. He died in London in 1791.		
1704	27	STANISLAV I	Poland	1709
1704		On August 2, the French and Bavarian armies were heavily defeated by the English forces and their allies, under John Churchill, first Duke of Marlborough, at Blenheim, on the river Danube in Bavaria.		
1705	9	JOSEPH I	Sicily, Germany, Hungary, HRE	1711
1706	17	JOHN V	Portugal	1750
1709		On July 8, PETER, 'The Great', of Russia vanquished the Swedish army, under CHARLES XII, at Pultowa.		
1711	27	CHARLES III	Sicily, Germany, Hungary, HRE	1740
1713	25	FREDERICK-WILLIAM I	Prussia	1740
1713	47	VICTOR AMADEUS II	Sicily, Naples, Sardinia	1730
1714	54	GEORGE I	Great Britain	1727
1715	5	LOUIS XV	France	1774
1717		On January 4, the *Triple Alliance* was ratified, whereby Great Britain, Holland and France were to be united against Spain.		
1718	30	ULRICA ELEANORA	Sweden	1720
1720	44	FREDERICK I	Sweden	1751
1725	46	CATHERINE	Russia	1727
1727	44	GEORGE II	Great Britain	1760
1727	12	PETER II	Russia	1730
1730	29	CHARLES-EMANUEL III	Sardinia	1773
1730	37	ANNE	Russia	1740
1730	31	CHRISTIAN VI	Denmark, Sweden, Norway	1746

Date of Accession	Age at Accession	Monarch	Kingdom(s)	Date Reign Ended
1733	37	AUGUSTUS III	Poland	1763
1734	18	CHARLES IV	Spain, Naples	1788
1740	0	IVAN VI	Russia	1741
1740	28	FREDERICK II	Prussia	1786
1740	24	MARIA THERESA	Hungary, Germany	1780
1741	32	ELIZABETH	Russia	1762
1742	45	CHARLES VII	HRE, Bohemia	1745
1745	37	FRANCIS	HRE	1765
1746	23	FREDERICK V	Denmark, Norway	1766
1746	34	FERDINAND VI	Spain	1759

1746	On March 31, the painter, Francisco Goya y Lucientes, was born near Saragossa. He died at Bordeaux in 1828.
1749	On August 28, Johann Wolfgang von Goethe was born at Frankfort. He died at Weimar in 1832.

1750	36	JOSEPH	Portugal	1777
1751	41	ADOLPH FREDERICK	Sweden	1771

1759	On September 13, General Wolfe defeated the French at Quebec and British rule was established in eastern Canada.

1759	8	FERDINAND I	Naples, Two Sicilies	1825
1759	43	CHARLES III	Spain, Two Sicilies	1788
1760	22	GEORGE III	Great Britain, Hanover	1820
1762	34	PETER III	Russia	1762
1762	33	CATHERINE II	Russia	1796

1763	FREDERICK, 'The Great', established village schools in Prussia.

1764	32	STANISLAV II (LK)	Poland	1795
1765	24	JOSEPH II (J)	HRE	1790
1766	17	CHRISTIAN VII	Norway, Denmark, Sweden	1808

1770	On December 16, Ludwig van Beethoven was born at Bonn. He died in Vienna, aged 57.

1771	25	GUSTAV III	Sweden	1792
1773	47	VICTOR-AMADEUS II	Sardinia	1796
1774	20	LOUIS XVI	France	1792

1776	On July 4, the *American Declaration of Independence* was carried by Congress. (New Orleans and the Louisiana Territory – named after LOUIS XIV – belonged to France, until America bought the land in April 1803).
1777	On October 17, the British Army (of 6,000 men) surrendered to the American General Gates at Saratoga.

1777	27	MARIA (J)	Portugal	1816
1780	39	JOSEPH II	Hungary, Austria	1790

122

Date of Accession	Age at Accession	Monarch	Kingdom(s)	Date Reign Ended
1784	16	FREDERICK VI	Denmark, Norway, Sweden	1839
1786	42	FREDERICK-WILLIAM II	Prussia	1797

| 1787 | | Sierra Leone, in Africa, was settled by English colonists. | | |

| 1788 | 40 | CHARLES IV | Spain | 1808 |
| 1790 | 43 | LEOPOLD II | Hungary, Austria, HRE | 1792 |

| 1791 | | In July the revolutionary *Reign of Terror* began in France. King Louis XVI was guillotined eighteen months later. | | |

| 1792 | 14 | GUSTAV IV | Sweden | 1809 |
| 1792 | 24 | FRANCIS I (LK) | Hungary, Austria, HRE | 1835 |

| 1792 | | On September 20, the French army, under Kellerman, defeated the Duke of Brunswick's Prussian forces at Valmy, in north eastern France. | | |

1793	8	LOUIS XVII	France	1795
1796	44	CHARLES-EMANUEL IV	Sardinia	1802
1796	42	PAUL	Russia	1801
1797	25	FREDERICK-WILLIAM III	Prussia	1840

| 1798 | | On August 1, Admiral Horatio Nelson destroyed the French Fleet at the *Battle of the Nile* (Aboukir). | | |

| 1799 | 32 | JOHN VI | Portugal | 1826 |

| 1800 | | The estimated population of Europe was 180 million. | | |

| 1801 | | On January 1, the *Union Jack* became the official flag of the United Kingdom of Great Britain, incorporating the crosses of Saints George, Andrew and Patrick. | | |

1801	24	ALEXANDER	Russia	1825
1801	28	LOUIS I	Etruria	1803
1802	43	VICTOR-EMANUEL I	Sardinia	1821
1803	14	LOUIS II	Etruria	1808
1804	35	NAPOLEON BONAPARTE	France	1815
1804	36	FRANZ I	Austria	1835
1805	49	MAXIMILIAN	Bavaria	1825
1805	51	FREDERIC I	Wurttemberg	1816
1806	56	FREDERICK AUGUSTUS I	Saxony	1827
1806	28	LOUIS BONAPARTE	Netherlands	1810
1806	38	JOSEPH BONAPARTE	Naples, Spain	1808
1807	23	JEROME BONAPARTE (LK)	Westphalia	1813
1808	40	FREDERICK VI	Denmark	1839
1808	37	JOACHIM MURAT	Naples	1815
1809	61	CHARLES VIII	Sweden, Norway	1818
1813	29	FERDINAND VII	Spain	1833

Date of Accession	Age at Accession	Monarch	Kingdom(s)	Date Reign Ended
1813		On May 22, Richard Wagner, composer, was born at Leipsic. He died in Venice in 1883.		
1814	60	LOUIS XVIII	France	1824
1815		On Sunday, June 18, the Allies, under the Duke of Wellington, defeated NAPOLEON's 72,000 strong army at Waterloo, in Belgium.		
1815	65	FERDINAND I	Naples, Two Sicilies	1825
1815	43	WILLIAM I	Netherlands	1840
1816	35	WILLIAM I	Wurttemberg	1864
1816	49	JOHN VI	Portugal	1826
1818	55	CHARLES XIV	Sweden, Norway	1844
1819		The *S.S. Savannah* a 350 ton ship *steamed* across the Atlantic in 26 days.		
1820	58	GEORGE IV	Great Britain, Hanover	1830
1821	56	CHARLES-FELIX	Sardinia	1831
1824	67	CHARLES X	France	1830
1825	39	LUDWIG I	Bavaria	1848
1825	58	FRANCIS I	Two Sicilies	1830
1825	29	NICHOLAS I	Russia	1855
1826	28	PEDRO IV	Portugal	1826
1826	7	MARIA	Portugal	1853
1827	62	ANTHONY	Saxony	1836
1828	26	MIGUEL	Portugal	1834
1829		The Nile rose 26 cubits (15.8 metres) during its annual flood, rather than the necessary minimum of 16 cubits and 30,000 Egyptians were drowned.		
1830	65	WILLIAM IV	Great Britain, Hanover	1837
1830	20	FERDINAND II	Two Sicilies	1859
1830	55	LOUIS XIX	France	1830
1830	10	HENRI V	France	1830
1830	57	LOUIS-PHILIPPE	France	1848
1830		On September 15, Huskisson, an English politician, became the first person in the world to be killed in a railway accident.		
1830	33	CHARLES-ALBERT	Sardinia	1849
1831	41	LEOPOLD I	Belgium	1865
1832	17	OTHO I	Greece	1862
1833	3	ISABELLA II	Spain	1870
1835	42	FERDINAND I	Austria	1848
1836	39	FREDERICK AUGUSTUS II	Saxony	1854
1837	66	ERNEST AUGUSTUS	Hanover	1851
1837	18	VICTORIA	Great Britain	1901

Date of Accession	Age at Accession	Monarch	Kingdom(s)	Date Reign Ended
1839		The fifty-year-old, Louis Jacques Mandé Daguerre perfected his photographic process.		
1839	53	CHRISTIAN VIII	Denmark	1848
1840	45	FREDERICK-WILLIAM IV	Prussia	1861
1844	48	WILLIAM II	Netherlands	1849
1844	45	OSCAR I	Sweden, Norway	1859
1847		Sir James Simpson first used chloroform as an anaesthetic.		
1848	18	FRANZ JOSEPH I	Austria	1916
1848	37	MAXIMILIAN II	Bavaria	1864
1848	40	FREDERICK VII	Denmark	1863
1849	32	WILLIAM III	Netherlands	1890
1849	29	VICTOR-EMANUEL II (LK)	Sardinia, Italy	1878
1851	32	GEORGE V (LK)	Hanover	1866
1852	44	NAPOLEON III (LK)	France	1870
1853	16	PEDRO V	Portugal	1861
1854	53	JOHN	Saxony	1873
1855	37	ALEXANDER II	Russia	1881
1859	23	FRANCIS II (LK)	Two Sicilies	1860
1859	33	CHARLES XV	Sweden, Norway	1872
1859		Charles Darwin published his revolutionary *Origin of Species by Natural Selection. Descent of Man* followed in 1871.		
1861	64	WILLIAM I (LK)	Prussia, German Empire	1888
1861	23	LUIS	Portugal	1889
1863	18	GEORGE I	Greece	1913
1863	45	CHRISTIAN IX	Denmark	1906
1863		The population of Lisbon was 224,000. In 1860 that of Athens was 47,000 and Copenhagen 155,000. In 1862 Naples was 418,000, Palermo 167,000, Madrid 475,000, Munich 167,000 and Vienna 560,000. In 1866, Warsaw was 243,000, Konigsberg 104,000, Brussels 189,000, Stockholm 138,000, Christiana (Oslo) 57,000 and Paris 1.8 million. In 1867, Amsterdam was 264,000, Dublin 319,000, Rome 215,000 and London 3 million.		
1864	41	CHARLES I	Wurttemberg	1891
1864	19	LUDWIG II	Bavaria	1886
1865	30	LEOPOLD II	Belgium	1909
1867		On June 19, the Emperor Maximilian of Mexico was shot, after trial, by the Mexicans. He was the brother of the Austrian Emperor and son-in-law of the King of Belgium.		
1869		On November 17, the Suez Canal was opened, bringing the Far East 'weeks nearer' to Europe.		

Date of Accession	Age at Accession	Monarch	Kingdom(s)	Date Reign Ended
1870	25	AMADEUS	Spain	1873
1872	43	OSCAR II	Sweden, Norway	1907
1873	45	ALBERT	Saxony	1902
1874	17	ALFONSO XII	Spain	1885
1878	34	UMBERTO I	Italy	1900
1881	36	ALEXANDER	Russia	1894
1881	42	CAROL	Romania	1914
1882	28	MILAN I	Serbia	1889
1885	27	MARIA CHRISTINA	Spain	1886

1885		Karl Benz built a single cylinder petroleum powered motor car engine.		

1886	0	ALFONSO XIII	Spain	1931
1886	38	OTTO	Bavaria	1913
1887	26	FERDINAND	Bulgaria	1918
1888	57	FREDERICK III	German Empire	1888
1888	29	WILLIAM II (LK)	German Empire	1918
1889	26	CHARLES	Portugal	1908
1889	13	ALEXANDER I	Serbia	1903
1890	10	WILHELMINA	Netherlands	1948
1891	43	WILLIAM II (LK)	Wurttemberg	1918
1894	26	NICHOLAS II (LK)	Russia	1918

1895		Guglielmo Marconi invented Wireless Telegraphy. Wireless messages were transmitted from England to Newfoundland in 1901.		

1900		The estimated population of Europe was 390 million.		

1900	31	VICTOR-EMANUEL III	Italy, Albania (LK)	1946
1901	59	EDWARD VII	Great Britain	1910
1902	70	GEORGE	Saxony	1904

1903		On December 17, the Wright brothers made the first successful flight in a petrol-engined aeroplane.		

1904	39	FREDERICK-AUGUSTUS III	Saxony (LK)	1918
1905	33	HAAKON VII	Norway	1957
1906	63	FREDERICK VIII	Denmark	1912
1907	49	GUSTAV V	Sweden	1950
1908	19	MANUEL II (LK)	Portugal	1910
1909	34	ALBERT I	Belgium	1934
1910	45	GEORGE V	Great Britain	1936
1912	42	CHRISTIAN X	Denmark	1947
1913	45	CONSTANTINE I	Greece	1917
1913	59	LUDWIG III (LK)	Bavaria	1918

1914		On June 28, Archduke Francis Ferdinand of Austria was assassinated at Sarajevo in Bosnia. This murder led to the outbreak of the First World War on August 4.		

1914	49	FERDINAND I	Romania	1927

Date of Accession	Age at Accession	Monarch	Kingdom(s)	Date Reign Ended
1914	38	WILLIAM I	Albania	1914
1916	29	KARL (LK)	Austria	1918
1917	23	ALEXANDER I	Greece	1920
1918	24	BORIS III	Bulgaria	1943
1918	74	PETER I	Yugoslavia, Serbia (LK)	1921
1921	33	ALEXANDER	Yugoslavia	1934
1922	32	GEORGE II	Greece	1947
1926		On January 26, John Logie Baird demonstrated his invention of television, in London.		
1927	6	MICHAEL (LK)	Romania	1947
1927		On May 20/21, Charles Lindbergh flew from New York to Paris in 37 hours.		
1928	33	ZOG I	Albania	1948
1930	37	CAROL II	Romania	1940
1934	33	LEOPOLD III	Belgium	1951
1934	11	PETER II (LK)	Yugoslavia	1945
1936	42	EDWARD VIII	Great Britain	1936
1936	41	GEORGE VI	Great Britain	1952
1939		On September 3, the United Kingdom and France declared war on Germany and the Second World War (second in 21 years) began.		
1943	6	SIMEON (LK)	Bulgaria	1946
1945		On August 6, America dropped an atomic bomb on Hiroshima, followed by a second, on Nagasaki, three days later. Japan surrendered unconditionally.		
1946	42	UMBERTO II (LK)	Italy	1946
1947	48	FREDERICK IX	Denmark	1972
1947	46	PAUL	Greece	1964
1948	39	JULIANA	Netherlands	1980
1950	62	GUSTAV VI	Sweden	1973
1950		The population of Europe was about 490 million. In 1975 it was about 635 million and the forecast for AD 2000 is in excess of 710 million.		
1951	54	OLAF V	Norway	
1951	21	BAUDOUIN	Belgium	
1952	26	ELIZABETH II	Great Britain	
1964	24	CONSTANTINE II (LK)	Greece	1967
1972	32	MARGARETHE	Denmark	
1973	27	CARL GUSTAV XVI	Sweden	
1975	27	JUAN CARLOS	Spain	
1980	42	BEATRIX	Netherlands	

127